To Al

Thanks for supporting us over the years!

Sincerely
Elyn & Nick
8/22/07

MW01164632

Horses for Courses

Horses for Courses

Adventures in Thoroughbred Racehorse Ownership

Dick Pollard

VANTAGE PRESS
New York

FIRST EDITION

All rights reserved, including the right of
reproduction in whole or in part in any form.

Copyright © 2007 by Dick Pollard

Published by Vantage Press, Inc.
419 Park Ave. South, New York, NY 10016

Manufactured in the United States of America
ISBN: 978-0-533-15637-5

Library of Congress Catalog Card No.: 2006908536

0 9 8 7 6 5 4 3 2 1

For Saratoga County—A Real Champion

With appreciation to Liane Crossley, our Kentucky contact,
for her knowledge of the horse business
and her technical assistance

Contents

Horses for Courses

1

How It All Began

Evelyn has always had a love for horses, but then so have many young women. Her major summer vacation spot was a dude ranch in upstate New York where she combined her interest in meeting boys with riding horses. I, on the other hand, grew up unaffected by contact with animals of any type, although I have a faint memory of a family cat.

When asked why they are buying thoroughbred horses, many potential owners give you a broad range of reasons ranging from "I've been betting on them for years and finally decided to try owning one" to "my family has been in the business for years." My reasoning leans closer to the former, although I'm not much of a gambler. Evelyn was extending her dude ranch days.

The one ingredient we lacked early on was money. If you believe in omens, we had one. We were both born in the same hospital at the same time. In those days mothers stayed for ten days, so we had adjoining bassinets for the last six days (makes Evelyn the older woman). Neither of our parents had much going for them financially. We missed the opportunity to be born into the kind of family that could buy us early entry into the sport of kings. Instead, we graduated from high schools in neighboring towns. Evelyn was the school's head cheerleader, I was the head nerd, but somehow we met each other again.

I was a bank clerk working in New York City. Evelyn was a secretary for an oil company big-wig in the same city. We met at an Irish American dance. (She's Irish, I'm an American.) We went through several small houses and raised two children, while I spent seven years getting a college degree at night. In the mid-seventies my career path took me from New York to Massachusetts, where I joined a small Boston-based bank holding company as the senior lending officer. It was there we first sunk our roots into the horse business.

Loaning money to commercial enterprises requires a thorough knowledge of the business requesting the financing. As an example, when I was a major lender to the shipping industry, I found myself seeing life through the eyes of a ship owner. My customers ranged from the famous Greek shipping magnates to the owner of a family towboat. It was necessary that I become an industry expert, so I found myself testifying in Washington on shipping issues and serving on blue ribbon commissions involving ocean-born transport.

Upon moving to Boston, I became involved with a new set of customers and industries. One of them was Edward G. Leroux, Jr., better known as Buddy. His business was sports medicine, deal making, and eventually, horse racing. This is where we were introduced to the world of thoroughbred horse ownership.

To get the flavor of this important turning point in our lives, it's necessary to spend a little time with Buddy. He was a local kid, an entrepreneur who had the ability to see and understand vertical integration in everything he did. He often told the story of one of his first business ventures. Buddy owned a broken-down garbage truck operating in his neighborhood, and he soon realized that a small herd of garbage-eating goats in his backyard was a natural extension of his operation. This approach eventually flowered into a major rehabilitation hospital that fed directly into congregate living units. The only thing missing was a cremation service.

My first real contact with Buddy was his request for financing to buy the Red Sox. With the death of Tom Yawkey, the estate had the team and its famous stadium, Fenway Park, up for sale. As usual, Buddy wasn't bringing much personal wealth to the deal, but he had brought together several important people who saw the potential profitability of the venture (in support of their perception just trace the current value of major league baseball franchises). As Donald Trump would say in *The Art of the Deal*, buying the Red Sox required a lot of imagination. The league would not accept a new owner borrowing money to make the purchase, so Buddy had to call on a lifetime of contacts developed during his years as a trainer for a number of major teams in various sports. By my lending to them directly, supported by their personal assets, Buddy was able to generate enough direct investment cash to make the deal go. His ownership group consisted of Tom Yawkey's wife, Haywood Sullivan, an ex-Red Sox player, and Buddy. As with most things in his life, the adventure had just begun.

Now Buddy's vertical integration instincts came into full bloom. He started a congregate living operation in Winterhaven, Florida, the spring training home of the Red Sox. He developed his own airline, Allstar Airlines, to transport his players and players of other pro sports teams from city to city. He formed a broadcasting company to sell a sports venue to the New England market, and best of all, he put a group together to buy Suffolk Downs. The track had a prime location, just outside of Boston, on a subway line. Part of his vision was a future stadium site for the Red Sox, which would allow him to sell the downtown property under Fenway Park. (Let it be noted that the park is still there and Suffolk hasn't moved.) The fact that not all Buddy's visions materialized was probably good news to many Bostonians.

At the same time, he bought land and built a horse farm on the side of a mountain in New Hampshire, near his summer house. He also bought a nursery and a supermarket in the same area. (Does the expression money burning a hole in your pocket come to mind?)

Money wasn't exactly burning a hole in our pocket, but the industry knowledge I had to gain to follow Buddy's entrance into the thoroughbred business awoke an interest in us. He had broodmares, foals, and yearlings on his farm. He shipped to Kentucky to get his mares in foal and they were born at his Winner's Circle farm in New Hampshire (about the closest any of his horses ever came to a real winner's circle). In fact, in his new house on the farm, he built a huge trophy case, and the last time I saw the case, it housed one small trophy.

The seed had been planted, however, and Evelyn got herself a cheap yearling. Buddy introduced us to his trainer, who many years later was described to us as "not being able to train a rat to go to cheese." (A possible reason why Buddy's trophy case was so empty.) The horse was also the subject of Evelyn's first incisive horse observation, "Why is he limping?" Needless to say, the horse never raced. Undeterred, we shook off our first negative experience and purchased another yearling, naming her Jen's Trueheart and thereby acquiring the foundation mare of Evelyn's horse empire.

As for Buddy, he continued to make deals, and get into new businesses with a multitude of partners. Sports medicine flourished as an industry and my financing focused on that area of his operation, while other institutions banked his more adventurous ventures. Thanks to our newly acquired knowledge of thoroughbred racing and sports franchises, we were able to avoid the inevitable downslide of Buddy's fortunes. As I recall, the personal banking division of a large New York City institution "stole" the business away from me.

One side effect of all this was that I spent more time at Suffolk Downs and Rockingham Park in New Hampshire than a reputable banker should have. Another of my interests, at the time, was community relations. As the Chairman of the Board of the Massachusetts Banker's Association I had the responsibility of dealing with a minority community unhappy with the way local banks appeared to be handling their mortgage business. It was a task requiring a good deal of give and take, and reliance on interpersonal relationships. I recall one of the more vocal activists, employed by the hotel workers' union, calling to tell me that his people spotted me at the track when I was supposed to be hard at work in Boston. My reply was that since my reputation in the minority community was one of being a regular guy, not a stuffy banker, I suggested that he publish the information far and wide. He didn't. (More about community activists later.)

Another side activity was my role as Chairman of Boston Ballet. The connection with horse racing, as many people subsequently pointed out, was a preoccupation with legs. Always interested in public relations, we named one of our homebreds Boston Ballet and used the tape of his first win at Suffolk Downs as a fund-raising tool for the ballet.

As our thoroughbred interests grew, Buddy's fortunes continued to decline. The bank had a luxury suite behind home plate where we entertained customers. He, in turn, had his own suite down the hall from ours. Because of his notoriety, I encouraged him to drop in whenever he could because my customers loved it. He was clever, he was colorful, he was Buddy. When I dropped in on his suite, the room was filled with sports celebrities and local business people, allowing me to make contacts of my own. Haywood Sullivan, with a suite next to Buddy, usually couldn't match his crowd. As his problems increased, I could detect a decline in his popularity, and it got to the point where he was no longer the customer favorite he had been. I remember dropping in on Buddy one night and finding him alone. He asked if there was anyone in our suite and I replied, "Nobody that wants to meet you." (Such are the ups and downs of the business world.) Evelyn and I have learned, subsequently, to roll with those kinds of punches. The final straw came when Haywood had the door handle removed from Buddy's side of their connecting suites. One might say that Buddy went from the toast of the town to just plain toast.

When the dust settled, Fenway Park was still in downtown Boston, Suffolk Downs and the Red Sox were under new management, Buddy was still making deals, and Evelyn and I were about to buy the farm.

2

Buying the Farm

Recalling her dude ranch days, Evelyn signed up for a weekly riding session at a local horse farm. It was the early eighties and we were spending some time in New Hampshire living right across the lake from Buddy Leroux's Winner's Circle Farm.

At this point, Slate Ledge Pride joined our life. He was a big, old quarter horse with a checkered past that included a winning career on the horse show circuit and a trip to Hawaii accompanied by a nasty cowboy type who abandoned him there. He eventually found his way back to the mainland and ended up giving rides to little children and an aging dude rancher in New Hampshire. His attitude was generally benign. He looked at the world through the eyes of a horse who had seen it all—the good, the bad, and the ugly.

His new rider, Evelyn, seemed friendly enough, although she had some trouble putting on his tack. On the plus side, she was not much heavier than the kids he had gotten used to.

That summer we decided to tour some horse areas, primarily Lexington, Kentucky, and Ocala, Florida. We wanted to nurture the spark of interest that Buddy had struck.

Lexington was quite an eye-opener. We hooked up with a young lawyer who specialized in the horse business and he introduced us to a local bloodstock agent with deep experience in the industry. We, apparently, looked like potential clients (it must have been the money hanging out of our pockets), so they arranged a tour of the big farms. We met the likes of Secretariat, Affirmed, Forty-Niner, Gulch, Dixieland Band, and Alysheba.

The latter stepped on Evelyn's pocketbook (a hoof mark that she never smoothed out). All the horses seemed to have the same "we've seen it all" attitude, portrayed by Slate Ledge Pride. It was true, of course, that as far as the horse business is concerned, they had all seen a heck of a lot more than Evelyn and I.

In addition to discovering that all the women in Lexington are named Muffy and Buffy, we came away with a spark that had turned into a small flame.

By the time we reached Ocala our plans included a real estate agent. We decided to get an early jump on my retirement date. Our approach to buying real estate had always been quite unique. I can't ever remember not buying the first property we saw, and it turned out the same way in Ocala. It doesn't mean we stop looking at other offerings. What happens is Evelyn goes into her "uh huh" mode. Every feature of every farm shown her after the initial one got "uh huhd" until the agent lost interest and started negotiating on a price for the first property.

We thought the purchase over for about a minute and whipped out our checkbook. At this point we began the naming debate. We settled on Richlyn Farm (a clever combination of our first names) and moved on to consider how we could appear bigger than we really were. Richlyn Farms gave the impression that we were a chain of farms. Richlyn Farm South implied that there was a North.

Regardless of the grand naming plans, the farm had only fifteen acres with a nice house and a ten-stall barn. In picturing our life there we envisioned Slate Ledge Pride holding sway in the paddocks. (We had, by this time, decided he was to be part of our family.) The property was quite a distance from the main road in an enclave that included two other bigger parcels, one of which was retained by the woman who sold us our farm. This was a relationship that we ended up regretting and led us to buy her out several years later.

The problem we now faced was finding someone to run the farm with Evelyn while I beat a hasty retreat back to Boston and the comparative serenity of community relations bickering and ballet fund raising. The problem solved itself when Nancy, Buddy's broodmare manager, arrived. She had grown tired of delivering foals on the side of a mountain in New Hampshire and decided to ply her trade in sunny Florida.

The first equine arrival (officially making it a one-horse farm) was, of course, Slate Ledge Pride. He climbed out of the van with a "it ain't Hawaii, but it ain't bad" look in his eye. After roaming through the paddocks and selecting his stall, he set to work figuring out how to help these two confused women.

Because it was Florida and there were fairly wide open spaces, the first thing the confused women did was arm themselves. Evelyn's choice was a well-balanced thirty-eight-caliber pistol, which was followed by a strategically placed sign reading, "This property protected by Smith and Wesson."

Being good citizens, they quickly signed up for a police gun class. Sergeant Otto, running the class, fielded Evelyn's first question which was, "Otto—what if someone breaks into my house?" He answered, "Evelyn—shoot him and call me." She countered, "Otto—what if I run into him outside?" He answered, "Evelyn—shoot him, drag him inside the house, and call me." (Such are the adventures on the frontier.)

Although the ladies were now prepared to handle any danger that came through the formidable front gates to the farm, they were unprepared for someone stealing the gates.

But sure enough, when Evelyn went down to open them one morning, they were gone. Even Otto didn't have a solution for this (no one for Evelyn to shoot). Such thefts usually show up at the local auction house, but they weren't very helpful, and going from farm to farm examining the gates didn't seem like a great idea. Instead, Evelyn took on a new crusade, illuminating the gate area.

Thus began Evelyn's new adventure with the local service provider. She quickly discovered that the electric lines ran through the back fields and not down the main road, making it difficult to illuminate the gate and the long road to the farm. She initiated a campaign that would take a long time to bear fruit.

The local electric co-op got to know her very well as she continued to pursue her request. They pointed out that a quarter mile of electric poles would be very expensive and they could hardly be covered by the her monthly utility payments. It was then they discovered what I already knew— Evelyn never gives up. It wasn't until she called the president of the co-op and said those magic words, "you wouldn't treat me this way if I were a man" that she won the battle.

Evelyn and Nancy sat down by the road that night with a bottle of champagne and raised a toast when the lights along our road and the gate went on.

While the women in his life were arming themselves and fighting with the electric co-op people, Slate was content to be the farm big shot. The lady on the adjoining parcel had registered complete disgust when he first exited the van (she had expected a thoroughbred). Slate, however, knew he was smarter than her and would eventually prove it. He got to show his smarts when Evelyn loaned him to a local member of the Ocala horse patrol for a big local event. Slate caught our neighbor in the crowd making disparaging remarks about his manhood, and he darn near trampled her. She shouted, "I know that horse, he's crazy" (crazy like a fox).

Slate's role as the boss of the farm came under siege with the arrival of Jen's True Heart, Evelyn's foundation mare, and a newly purchased quarter horse named Angel. We began our chosen business as a breeding farm by attempting to get our new females in foal. Slate also launched his new career as a teaser. As you might expect, he really loved it. After he got a testosterone shot (not that he really needed one), his job was to parade around in front of the mares and determine their readiness for breeding. He had that "now you're talking" look in his eye when we introduced him to his new profession.

Richlyn Farm had come to a crossroad. Were we breeding quarter horses or thoroughbreds or both? (Slate didn't get a vote.) Were we going to buy a select group of expensive mares and breed them to expensive stallions or just fill up the barn? The latter decision was significant because by that time we had bought out our annoying neighbor and added twenty stalls plus a manager's house and employee apartments (we were rapidly taking on the grand scale we had envisioned). Another question was whether we were breeding for racing or selling or both?

With all these decisions we were smart enough to ask the advice of some local, veteran horsemen, and of course, dumb enough to ignore their advice if it differed with our grand plan. The size decision was influenced by the growth of our facility and the enthusiasm of our farm manager. We launched our program of buying relatively cheap mares (all thoroughbreds). We bred them to lower priced, local stallions and looked to sell them as yearlings in Ocala's annual sales.

Launching a barn-filling operation without a huge pot of money required some clever buying. In addition, after the babies started arriving, naming them involved a great deal of imagination. Also, a full barn required more help and I found myself handling tougher personnel problems than I faced during my years as personnel director of the Chase Manhattan Bank.

3

Filling Up the Farm

Once the decision was made to fill up the barns, the next step was to attend the Ocala mixed sales, which featured mares in foal. That option provided us with a two-fer. We could buy a broodmare and add a foal in a relatively short period of time. Some foals are actually delivered at the sale or shortly before and the foals followed their mothers into the sales ring.

Our first purchase still sticks in my mind. We settled on a King Emperor mare named Court Card who was in foal to Fight Over, a moderately priced stallion. When the hammer came down, we had made our first buy for the grand sum of $2,500, and we could not have been more pleased.

Horse auctions are seductive. Over the next several years, we enjoyed the process of gathering our broodmare band. Since we were not buying at the high end of the market, luck played a role. A broodmare picks up or loses value as her progeny perform on the racetrack. As an example, we were bidding on a dispersal of several big, gray Al Hattab mares from the barn of a well-known conditioner. We settled on one of them, only to be outbid by Kinsman Farm, George Steinbrenner, proprietor. They bought her for $15,000 and we proceeded to buy another mare from that group. A year later, while I was watching a simulcast, I noticed a two-year-old named Holy Bull blow a very good field of allowance horses away. His dam was Sharon Brown, the mare we were the underbidder on. Kinsman Farm had added more value to an already very successful operation.

The phenomenon of mares taking on the value of their progeny was driven home to us years later when one of our homebreds, a nasty but talented colt named Kachemak Bay ran in the Pilgrim Stakes against one of the best grass horses in the country. King Cugat, syndicated by Centennial Farms and ridden by Jerry Bailey, was going off at less than even money. Our colt had just won for the first time in his career at the Meadowlands and was bet at a very unflattering 29 to 1. I remember our lack of interest in going up to New York. We were in Florida at the time. We watched at Calder Race Course and hoped for a small piece of the purse at best. Our expectations began rising when it appeared that we had a lock on fifth, then fourth, then third, then second, and much to our surprise, he streaked on past King Cugat at the wire.

What was interesting was the reaction of the young guy who was running the farm at the time. He traced down the buyers of Kachemak Bay's mare, Snow Colony, whom we had sold several months earlier. He made an offer to purchase her to the current owner, who had not yet heard about the race. Needless to say, our guy resold the mare at a good price thanks to her enhanced resume. It was a good example of how one race can quickly affect the value of other horses represented in that race.

As the farm continued to fill up with mares and babies, Slate Ledge Pride presided over his kingdom. We put him in a paddock that adjoined our house, right by the bedroom window, where he could check to see if Evelyn was in bed before making his nightly rounds. Those rounds, unfortunately, included letting various horses out of their stalls. He had easily developed a system for opening the latch on his stall and he was soon busy opening other doors. We were perplexed by all the stray mares and weanlings we found in the morning and decided to stay up one night and watch. Sure enough, there was Slate, after checking on Evelyn, or what he thought was Evelyn in her bed, working his magic on the stall doors. All the latches were Slate-proofed after that night.

Horses being where they were not supposed to be was not always Slate's doing. We had a foal that was taken away from her mare at birth and had to be hand-fed. The baby remained healthy but grew up thinking that Evelyn might just be his mother. So much so that he had the run of the farm until he found his way into our house where we found him standing in the living room.

Another challenge, posed by the large collection of weanlings, was the naming process. Most farms selling their horses will leave them unnamed so the buyers can do the honors (even if they are named, the buyer can change the name at a nominal cost). We liked the idea of following the horse's progress if no changes were made.

The first baby we named was the Fight Over colt from our first mare purchase. Some foals come out with a burst of energy, others sneak out quietly. This one leaped up and bounced off the wall several times, knocking himself silly, but not doing any real damage (except to the wall). Nancy came up with his name right on the spot—Bonkers Over You. Note the clever use of the word Over from the sire Fight Over. Lest you think Nancy's rationale was a little weak, let me introduce a primer on naming horses.

1. Name the horse after its sire—This approach is particularly applicable when you paid a big stud fee and you want to brag about it. As an example, horses with cat in their names from the Storm Cat family ($500,000 stud fee). Or, as in our case, the Over family.

2. Name the horse after the mare—This is quite popular with mare owners who want to keep her name alive.

3. Name the horse after both the sire and the mare—This is the biggest favorite because it appeals to the imagination of the owners and shows how clever they really are. The second foal out of Court Card was sired by Mr. Frisky and was named Frisky's Wild Card (not too clever, but better than Bonkers Over You).

4. Include the owners name (s) in the name—The height of conceit, but probably OK if the husband is naming the horse after his wife. Jen's True Heart's first two foals were by Shot Gun Scott and were named Shot Gun Evie and Shot Gun Rich. The former gave us our first win (wouldn't you know).

5. Set a goal for the horse in the name—Silly if it doesn't work out. Our horse Rapid Fire wasn't rapid and never fired (not even once).

6. Bring your favorite institution into the name—Remember Boston Ballet. We also named Emerson Hall after Emerson College, where I was once a trustee. I remember giving a long explanation to the Jockey Club about Ralph Waldo Emerson being dead (you can't name a horse after a live person without getting permission).

7. Name the horse after a place—A very popular approach because it shows how well traveled you are and makes you look good to the people in the area you name. We used a bunch of streets early on. Rutland Road and Regis Road (both streets we had lived on) and Left on Nelson (in Saratoga, near the track, because Nelson Avenue was taken).

Number seven became our ultimate system of choice. After naming thirty or so horses, we tired of the name game. You would be surprised how many of your first choices have already been used (Bonkers Over You was not taken).

16

Most of our horses are now named after counties with some bays thrown in for the sake of variety. However, the final test of a name is how it sounds on the loudspeaker as your horse is charging down the stretch on the lead. Remember Man O' War. Jen's True Heart, although a cute little filly, would never cut it. Maybe that's why we never ran her.

Having made good progress in filling up the stalls and naming the foals, we turned our attention to hiring an appropriate number of high quality, reliable people to back up Evelyn and Nancy. (We failed and decided to settle for what we could get.) Hiring and keeping good people is the biggest challenge in the horse industry.

I wasn't a very big help, showing up on weekends and pretending to be a real horse farm guy. Our infamous next-door neighbor always said that she could tell I arrived by the number of different motor sounds arising from our side of the fence line. If I didn't act the part, at least I looked the part out on my big Ford tractor dragging the paddocks and mowing the grass fields. In fact, every salesman who happened up our road would ask me what the owners were like and if could he sell them anything. I always said, "Sure—especially that cute little woman, she's a real patsy." The farrier on his regular visit would ask how Juan the gardener was doing. I was no substitute for full-time help, so Nancy began an interview schedule.

The farm employment agency sent them over and we went through the applicants fairly quickly. The final decision was usually made by Slate, who could tell a floor flusher a mile away (from his own lifetime experiences). Among our more memorable employees were:

The little, old beer-drinking lady. Looked like your grandmother—drank like a sailor. We could always find her by following the trail of empty cans.

The guy with the wooden leg who had some problem with the more physical tasks.

The young couple with the snake. We wondered why the heat was on in their apartment during the summer.

The Frenchman with his own farm who took our feed home every night.

Norman, the kid who made the timely sale of Snow Colony and eventually managed the farm when Nancy left and ended up taking our horses to New England to race (in other words—he was the one hire who stuck).

Norman's uncle who helped me rid the farm of termite evidence so that we could sell it.

The nudist whom we hired to take care of the empty farm until we could get rid of it. We didn't know about her avocation until the real estate agent complained that every time she brought over a prospective buyer our overseer was without clothes. This appeared to be particularly annoying when she was riding the tractor (especially over bumpy ground). Norman's uncle began dating her and they eventually conspired to sell a lot of our furniture and keep the money.

All in all a fairly typical string of employees.

4

Breeding Business

During our years running a broodmare farm, we were singled out by one of the breeders' associations as an example of a successful small farm. A group of potential breeders was brought over to examine our operation. Evelyn and Nancy kept me as far away as they could from the group lest I verbalize my true feelings about the profitability of our venture, and the pitfalls involved.

Don't get me wrong, the pluses outweighed the minuses, but the pluses were hard to quantify. We loved watching our horses in the fields. We got great satisfaction tracking the growth and maturation of the weanlings and generally enjoyed being in the heart of the horse business. As an example, the mares had a society of their own. Given the freedom of wandering in the paddocks with each other, they quickly separated into leaders and followers. They staked out territories and chose friends and acquaintances. New mares entered the society at their own risk and called on all their political skills to gain a spot in the hierarchy. When Evelyn and Nancy picked out mares at the sales, all of this had to be considered. They, many times, rejected perfectly good prospects on the strength of a perceived inability to get along with the crowd.

The economics of the business allowed very little downtime in the breeding cycle. Mares have an eleven-month gestation period, and one of the main goals was to produce foals earlier and earlier each year. This is especially true if you buy a mare carrying a late foal. Early birth dates make yearlings more attractive when they go to sale. More mature yearlings are able to run earlier as two-year-olds. The whole process of catching a mare in heat, getting her in foal with one breeding, birthing a baby properly, and keeping the young foal healthy is very complicated and frustrating.

Ocala is one of the country's premier breeding areas, helped by a large population of stallions standing at stud. Prices are, for the most part, fairly low and a good number of mares are available each year. The popular stallions usually have a waiting list and fitting the breeding into your mare's cycle is tricky. The window of availability can be quite small and the risk of missing a whole month is very real. Once covered, the wait to see if the mare is in foal is nerve-racking. If the vet declares she's not in foal, the process starts all over again. The worst-case scenario is for a mare to go through the whole breeding season and emerge barren.

As an aside, hanging around a breeding farm can get you labeled as a social misfit, if not a male chauvinist. Back in Boston, dealing with female business associates and referring to those who were pregnant as being "in-foal" never went over very big.

Evelyn enjoyed the birthing process. She had confidence in Nancy, who was really good at handling broodmares. I avoided it as much as possible. Nights when one of our mares was due to deliver Evelyn would lay out her clothes carefully for quick response. It reminded me of my earlier days in the Rockville Centre, New York, Volunteer Fire Department. The ring of the call box in my bedroom would galvanize me into quick action. The first person to the fire house got to drive the truck, and more importantly, they would hand off the equipment to the latecomers who had to plunge into the burning building (I wasn't much of a burning building guy).

Nancy would call Evelyn and the two of them would wrestle the baby away from the mare, trying not to injure either of them. By the time I dragged myself to the barn, the foal was usually careening around the stall looking for the mare's nursing equipment. Some found it quickly, others (read Bonkers Over You) took their time and dented many walls in the process.

Most births work out well even with all the commotion going on. It's the occasional problem that sticks in your mind. We had a newly purchased mare whose early milk contained poison that caused the death of the foal. Subsequent babies from that mare had to be separated and hand-fed until the milk became non-toxic. One of her later foals went on to win a big stakes race, proving the unusual handling of the birth and the early hand-feeding didn't impair the ability of the baby. All in all, broodmares and their foals proved to be a hearty lot.

From a financial point of view, a breeding farm is a long trail of expenses with no income until the yearlings make it to the auction ring. A successful birth is just the beginning. Next you must help the weanling grow into an attractive yearling who will catch the eye of a potential buyer.

The sales were always challenging. Most of our yearlings had very little, if any, exposure to life outside of the farm. Now we were asking them to get into a van and ship to a new stall in a strange barn surrounded by strange horses and stared at by a bunch of strange people. They would wander up, catalogues in hand, and ask to see one of our hip numbers (named that because of the small piece of tape with the catalogue number firmly affixed to the horse's rump). For each looker, the yearling is led out to walk up and down and be scrutinized by potential buyers, who may or may not know what their looking at. The horses that pass muster will attract one of the roving vets who are hired to stick tubes down the horse's throat to check its windpipe, or vets with x-ray equipment to look for bone problems. A popular yearling is pretty much beat-up by the time it reaches the sales ring. Some of the more aggressive horses tend to get really nasty by the end of the day. The amount of attention a yearling gets helps to set the reserve price, which can be adjusted right up to the time it enters the ring. As I recall, overly popular yearlings for which we set high reserve prices were something we didn't have to deal with very often.

We were gathering some real experience in both auction buying and selling. The former is proactive while the latter is sitting with your fingers crossed awaiting your fate. The worst feeling on the selling side is to have the hammer come down just below your reserve price and know that you will be paying a commission on a horse you didn't sell.

A horse unsold at the yearling sale can be broken, trained, and offered at next year's two-year-olds-in-training sale. That auction offered a new anxiety since part of the product appeal is the way a horse runs and how quickly it can complete an eighth or a quarter mile. If the horse still doesn't sell, you have pretty much run out of options and it's time to consider the racing business. We shipped our first non-seller north to New England and began to think about running more of our horses. We were tired of trying to scrape a profit out of the breeding industry and began to think about full-time racing (we figured we would lose the same amount of money, but have more fun doing it).

5

Racing off the Farm

Our first horse to work her way through the sales process and end up on the track was Shot Gun Evie. Proudly carrying Evelyn's name, she got nowhere near enough money at the yearling sale. We set the reserve at a level that would make Evelyn look good, but the buyers didn't seem to care.

Battered but unbowed, we put Shot Gun Evie through the training regimen and prepared her to run in the under-tack show. It is actually quite exciting to watch your horse coming around the turn and heading for the finish line with its timing display. Depending on whether you are an optimist or a pessimist, you feel that your horse is either running fast or slow, but the figure flashing up on the screen is the one you have to live with. Most auctions will give you a chance to try it one more time and you must decide if you want to stand pat or try another run several days later. For their part, the exercise riders are trying to get the fastest time without looking like they're working too hard.

We stood pat, got a price that befitted her namesake, and declared our first sale a success. But not quite. The buyer brought the horse home and found a minor physical problem that he didn't want to live with. Most sales now include repositories where consignors file x-rays for buyers to consult before the horse goes through the ring. It would be quite expensive to x-ray every horse you might be interested in (especially at the price level we were involved with). After a bit of give-and-take, the buyer, a northeastern trainer, agreed to take the horse with the right to return her if she could not train well. Apparently, she didn't, and Shot Gun Evie appeared on our doorstep a month later. As a final insult, the buyer refused to pay the van bill even though he had shipped her up the East Coast. So we had to pony-up to get Evelyn's horse back (excuse the pun). The problem was minor and we healed her up. She was soon heading back up north to run under our colors.

While Evelyn was fighting the farm battles, I was back in Boston setting up a racing team. The requirement was to find an honest and effective trainer (not all that easy). After asking around, I found a guy who was described as being very, very neat. Sensing neat would be high on Evelyn's list, I met him and liked him. His wife was a lawyer and his father had been in the horse business for years. We shipped Shot Gun Evie his way. Doing all this important horse business cost me some time away from the bank, but my secretary became really good at covering and I was careful not to make important phone calls from Suffolk Downs when a race was about to be called on the loudspeaker system. To further cement our racing posture in New England, we bought a small piece of a syndicate that eventually became a minority ownership in Suffolk Downs (without Buddy Leroux). The checking out, including fingerprints, was more than I ever received as a banker disbursing large loans, financing ocean-going shipping and major league baseball teams.

All this effort was finally rewarded. In June of 1996, after finishing on the board in her first race, Shot Gun Evie, with Joe Hampshire aboard, won her first race. The winner's circle included Evelyn (back from Florida for the summer) and a host of bankers playing hooky. We were on our way to stardom (or so we thought).

Meanwhile, Shot Gun Rich, anxious to do for his namesake what Shot Gun Evie had done for hers, was growing up down on the farm. Emboldened by our success with his sister, we made no attempt to sell him. Instead we had him broken and trained and prepared to enter the racing business. He came under the tutelage of an ex-jockey turned trainer. Our new conditioner had an interesting background, which included riding at the smaller less well-known tracks when he was breaking in. The stories of his early career brought home to us what small town racing was like. He described a run of wins he had at one time, which began to make him believe he was the second coming of Eddie Arcaro. Upon arriving in town, he was given a bunch of washed-up horses that he quickly turned into winners, at big prices. One day, at the height of his newly found prowess, he chanced to look back and he saw eight other jockeys frantically holding back their mounts so that he could win. (Those were the good old days.)

Anxious to make it as a trainer, he talked us into shipping Shot Gun Rich to Gulfstream Park to race. He packed our horse into his gooseneck trailer and loaded up his wife and Evelyn for the trip to Hallandale. On the way, they stopped at a parkway service plaza for lunch. Afterwards, they went out the northbound exit of the building rather than the southbound one and thought that someone had stolen Shot Gun Rich. In retrospect, it might have been a good thing.

I was up in New England, planning to watch the race on one of the off-track betting television screens at Suffolk Downs, not realizing what a trauma Evelyn had been going through. It seems that our training couple usually stays at a local motel near the track in an area not to be confused with Boca Raton. A group of backside employees were having a barbecue under her window and the room was not exactly up to her neatness standards. She locked the window, barricaded the door and slept fully clothed in a chair all night.

The next day, watching the race at Suffolk, I was presented with a strange sight in the saddling paddock. An exhausted looking Evelyn was standing next to an Indian woman (the trainer's wife had decided to dress early, early American, for the big race).

The trainer was there with a confused-looking female jockey. Julie Krone's agent had put her on this shipper from Ocala with an unknown trainer. She was wearing the wrong silks probably hoping it was the wrong horse. It wasn't. She rode Shot Gun Rich and came in tenth. Julie had that look in her eye indicating she didn't know why she was riding him, but at least she avoided getting hurt. An inauspicious beginning for a horse that was supposed to immortalize my name.

Shot Gun Rich went on to a long, but not particularly profitable, career in New England. He won his share of races, but never covered his costs. I remember the track program commenting, "Shot Gun Rich finally found his way to Rockingham Park, stopping in every gun shop along the way." (Not very funny, but the horse couldn't read.) He was eventually claimed for $5,000 and raced until he was eight. He closed his ninety-eight race career with eleven wins, but only $70,458 in earnings.

We did not let our first encounter with live racing discourage us. After all Shot Gun Evie did all right. In fact, we started to think more about running our horses rather than selling them. Our returns from the sales barely covered the cost of the breeding operation. In addition, the risk of a mare missing her season and going barren was always there as were the risks of illness and injury to the weanlings who tended to be fearless in their early months. Add to that the risk every birth brought of some type of problem that would make the sale of the horse difficult. When I checked in from Boston every night, the good news was no news and the bad news ranged from annoying to devastating. I remember a public relations person from the breeding industry once asking me why we gave up on the business. I replied, "We weren't losing money fast enough, so we decided to try the racing side." (Another prophetic wise guy comment.)

With our long-range racing objectives in mind, we paid more attention to the stallions we bred to our mares. Instead of looking for the biggest bargain or the hottest, or soon to be hottest, sales-friendly stallion we could find, we started to consider the sires that could produce runners for us.

The neighboring farm was owned by an ex-banker who had moved to Ocala when his savings and loan operation ran into trouble. Florida offered all sorts of asset protection unavailable elsewhere. Evelyn often commented he had hundreds of acres and we had a paltry sixty. "You are both bankers," she would say. (My answer was always, there are bankers and there are bankers.) In any event, he was standing Theatre Critic, billed as the only son of Sadler's Wells, a big European grass sire, standing in Florida. I astutely figured that mating two all-grass pedigrees would produce a turf horse. We had a mare named Ballet Rouge, a horse we purchased for more than our usual cheap price, who was a stakes winner in Italy and a fast grass horse. We expected great things.

As an aside, having a grass horse is not necessarily a good thing. A fact that we were to discover in later years. A grass horse, who can only run on the turf, has severely limited opportunities. Every trainer whose horse has bombed out on the dirt, wants to try the turf. (Hope beats eternal.) The result, too many horses and too few races. Also, wet weather forces many races off the grass. In addition, turf tracks can get so beaten-up jockeys refuse to ride, and the northern part of the country has no grass races at all in the winter. Great reasons not to breed a grass horse, but we were new to the business and what did we know?

We trotted Ballet Rouge through the fence line and over to our neighbor for the breeding ritual, and she was soon in foal with our future grass contestant. He was born without a problem and we named him Ballet Critic (another clever combination of sire and mare names).

Slate Ledge Pride, always on the lookout for up-and-comers to take under his experienced wing, showed real interest in our new addition. When Ballet Critic was weaned away from his mother, we put him in an adjoining paddock where Slate, now sporting gray hairs on his face, could instruct him about life with the two-legged folks. I'm sure he pointed out how disciplined we were about feeding time, and how nice that badly dressed guy keeps the paddocks and the fields with his big Ford tractor. He must have also mentioned that someday he might inherit the paddock with the window to the cute little woman's bedroom.

As to the less pleasant things in Ballet Critic's future, he probably explained why he had to control himself when the farrier was wrestling with his feet, pounding nails into his hoofs, or when the vet insisted on shoving tubes down his throat or up his posterior. His best suggestion would be to feign illness if he hears the words "he's going to be fixed."

Slate watched proudly as his protégé received instruction on the bridle and saddle. Warned in advance, Ballet handled the experience with quiet dignity. He took to the bit quickly and was soon running in the back fields. His occasional stumbles confirmed his turf pedigree as his grass stride caught his foot on the uneven footing of the fields (nothing like toughening up a horse). He never lost his rider, however, remembering Slate's speech about it being the horse's job to keep the rider onboard, even if the mishap is the rider's fault. Slate recalled all the children and the aging dude rancher he had to carry around the riding oval.

While Ballet Critic was learning his lessons from four-footed and two-footed creatures, Evelyn and I started thinking about our future, which included my retirement date.

6

Retiring and Selling the Farm

Back in Boston, my retirement date was rapidly approaching. The date was not a specific one, but everyone (including me) was recognizing the last thing they needed was a sixty-plus loan officer who seemed to be more interested in the horse business than the banking business. My original bank had been acquired by the city's largest financial institution, Bank of Boston. The increase in the value of our stockholdings as a result of the merger added to the funds we had available to buy horses down in Florida. The strong banking team we had developed was either staying with the merged bank or moving on to greener pastures (you see how horses are working their way into my speech patterns). It looked like a good time for me to negotiate a retirement package. The new CEO was once a trainee at the Chase Manhattan Bank in New York City where he learned the lending business from me in my role as chief lending instructor. I had always been happy to take on teaching assignments, especially when the class was made up of young MBAs on their way to stardom. Later in my career, they had a habit of showing up as my boss with fond memories of the contribution I made to their success.

One of the reasons so many bank mergers were taking place at that time was the bad patch of lending problems that occurred in the mid-nineties. My original Boston bank suffered, as well, during that period, but managed to survive due to the really high caliber group of lending people we had assembled. It was these rough times that drove our neighbor down in Florida to seek refuge and produce the sire of Ballet Critic. We managed to survive waves of federal bank examiners, panicky senior management, and a terrible real estate market to end up as a viable acquisition candidate when the industry consolidated.

It is the tough times, especially in the business world, that test your mettle and develop your management skills. I recall thinking about Rudyard Kipling's poem at the time—"if you keep your head when all about you are losing theirs and blaming it on you." The guy running our bank fit the quote completely. He had always looked to his bank as the platform for his legacy. The chance that his lending people would bungle away his legacy drove him wild. Fortunately, I never cared to pin the world's opinion of me on the success or failure of a middle-sized bank in New England. Evelyn and I hoped to establish our legacy pursuing another venue, thoroughbred horse racing. (How's that for a warped outlook on life?) Time has proven our position to be the right one. After two more mergers, my original bank disappeared into the history of what is now the Bank of America. It, in a sense, never existed (comparable to the fourth dam on the pedigree page of a sales catalogue). We, on the other hand, used the funds that three bank mergers produced to invest in an industry with statistics and records that last forever.

My only real regret was to be leaving my role as the banking connection to the community activists. Although my financial background helped my transition to the horse business, it was my ability to work with people from different backgrounds and a variety of agendas that proved to be invaluable.

The same economic issues that faced the commercial real estate market were appearing on the residential side as well.

The black and Hispanic communities had long felt discriminated against by the banks, who appeared to be funneling their mortgage money into the more affluent, white areas in and around Boston. While the banks used credit quality as an excuse, the community activists saw it differently. About that time, the government produced a lending study which seemed to support the activists' point of view. I was the incoming chairman of the Massachusetts Bankers Association, and fell right into the line of fire. The community also focused on my bank as a major culprit, making it all very personal.

Just as I had to adjust my outlook on business management when dealing with people in the horse business, I also had to adjust when dealing with the community groups. It took me a while to adapt. During that period, our condo was picketed by bullhorn-toting activists who demanded I come down and face them. We were in New Hampshire at the time, but it didn't make us too popular with the other residents in our condo.

One of the big complaints involved the lack of cash machines and branches in the minority neighborhoods. When I finally convinced the branch administration side of our bank to open a new branch in that community, all I received from the press was a too little, too late response. I recall standing proudly in front of our new branch on opening day, when a TV news team roared up. They stuck a microphone in my face and an annoying female anchor asked me why it took so long.

When the tide of public opinion finally drifted our way, the Harvard Business School decided to write a case about the process. It was my first exposure to having part of my life published, and it was an interesting experience. Favorable resolution required getting all the banks in town on the same page. It also required that the community groups control their activists. They just loved to stir up trouble. It convinced me the best way to handle contentious situations is to keep your sense of humor and be able to laugh at yourself (an approach which really helped us in recent years). I remember a meeting where one of the bankers on our side of the table turned red and started sputtering. The activists seized the opportunity. (They do mad so much better than bankers.) Yelling at your trainer accomplishes very little either, and does nothing for your long-term relationship.

As I mentioned earlier, the image I attempted to portray during these troubled times was one of an unconventional banker who sees humor in their more strident positions, and seems to be an ordinary kind of guy. (Evelyn always thought I was pretty ordinary.) In other words, someone who would be more at home driving a big Ford tractor on the back forty. At the big celebration dinner, the leaders of the minority community were sitting with me on the podium. "Pollard," they said, "are you sure you're a banker? You don't look like those other guys. In fact, they don't even seem to like you." They didn't. That's why we figured it was about time to get out of town and pursue our future in the horse business.

Boston Ballet was less happy to see us go. I had managed to do some fairly good fund-raising. The Ballet ran an annual corporate family night at the "Nutcracker" at Christmas and I strong-armed my corporate customers to buy overpriced tickets for their friends and family. I also persuaded a group of local luminaries and sports stars (such as Bobby Orr) to get on stage with the dancers and make fools of themselves to the delight of the audience. After two years of this scenario, my tactics were getting a little tiresome and an uprising was in the wings. (Pardon the pun.) I had found another good reason to skip town. We left the Ballet with a bunch of money in a charitable remainder trust, tied to Evelyn's ultimate demise. (I figured since her mother lived to be 100, we weren't really giving up the money any time soon.)

With most of the people in Boston breathing a sigh of relief, I headed into retirement, not sure how Evelyn and Nancy would adapt to my full-time presence.

Back at the farm, they were busy preparing for my arrival. Although Slate perceived that the women were less than excited about my permanent return to Ocala, he, for one, was happy to see me. He missed all those machine sounds and the action around the paddocks. It was apparent, however, the farm wasn't going to cut it in the long run. We made the decision to sell out and use some of the proceeds to build up a racing stable.

We began the process of preparing the mares and the weanlings for sale, while setting up Nancy in a nice little farm outside of town. She took her favorite broodmare with her (Court Card, the mother of Bonkers Over You). Norman brought our potential racing stable together for their trip to New England and we all faced up to our biggest issue, finding a home for Slate Ledge Pride.

Slate seemed to have noticed the activity around the farm and didn't lay it all on the doorstep of my permanent arrival. He was happy his protege, Ballet Critic, was looking hale, hardy and well educated, but Slate was sad to see everything else going, especially the mares and his testosterone shot. He was now twenty-seven and we had no place to take him. After extensive inquiries, Evelyn found a young girl, whose mother worked at the Ocala Breeders' sales office who was interested in getting a horse of her own. Slate had come full circle, back to keeping young children safe and happy. The aging dude rancher wiped a tear from her eye and vowed to keep in touch with him. (She never did. Dealing with age and death in her animals was always tough for her to do.)

All of our mares sold and brought fairly low prices except for Snow Colony, who benefited from Kachemak Bay's win in the Gotham. (Frankly, we never paid much for them to begin with.) The weanlings went for somewhat better prices. Norman took the two-year-olds up to New England and Ballet Critic went to our big-time New York trainer, John Campo, Jr. (or at least big-time to us). It seemed like a good match. With all of Slate's training, we felt Ballet Critic could handle just about anyone.

John worked his way into our confidence by his handling of Ballet Critic's older brother, Boston Ballet, and the professional manner in which Kachemak Bay dispatched King Cugat in the Pilgrim. Unfortunately, Kachemak broke his leg in the Tropical Park Derby, his next start, and had to be euthanized (a great example of the ups and downs of the horse business). Just as you shouldn't give all the credit to a trainer for a winning horse, you shouldn't give him all the blame when a horse breaks down. Racing luck has so much to do with what happens on the track. Horses are, and always will be, delicate animals even with all their size and power.

Selling the property proved to be a challenge. We were planning to sell the farm as one unit, but it went in the two parcels that we originally bought. The nudist slowed the process down as did the termites. One prospective buyer brought in a termite-sniffing dog from Miami, but Norman's uncle and I outwitted him. We tried to increase the price by throwing in the furniture, but Norman's uncle and the nudist didn't leave enough to make any difference. A comparison of the sales price and the original cost showed a modest profit (the first we made in the horse business).

7

Claiming Game

Our homebreds started to disappear through injuries and sales. With no new horses coming off the farm, we turned to other avenues for acquiring runners. One of these avenues was claiming.

Horses entered in claiming races are available for purchase at the price designated in the race conditions. The system was designed, not for encouraging the sale of horses, but to keep the races competitive. Without it, a trainer would be free to enter a high-quality horse in a low-quality race and walk away with an easy purse. He can still run his horse in such a race; however, he runs the risk of losing the horse. Any trainer, backed by enough money in a horseman's account and the proper paperwork, can drop a claim slip in the racing office up until about fifteen minutes before the gates open. In fact, a number of trainers can opt to claim the same horse. After the race, they draw lots to see who gets the animal. The successful claimer owns the horse once the race begins. The previous owner gets whatever share of the purse the horse wins and the previous trainer gets the race results recorded in his stats. I recall once asking a trainer to claim back a horse we had owned. The tag (claiming price) was $10,000, below the price at which we lost him. After the race, which we did not see, the message from our conditioner was good news and bad news. The good news was our claim had been successful. The bad news was that the horse was dead. He had broken down during the race and been euthanized. We were not only out the claiming price, but we had to dispose of the horse as well.

The soundness question separates claiming from a straight purchase. In the latter case, a full vet check can be performed so the buyer knows exactly what type of physical specimen is being purchased. Not so in claiming. It's let the buyer beware. A good claiming trainer relies on his ability to detect potential problems from afar. Many times, the claiming trainer will follow the horse to the saddling paddock to see how he walks, or at least, examine him very closely in the ring. They are also experts on diagnosing the reason for a class drop (from allowance to claiming or from one price level to a lower one).

Many times, a filly with a good pedigree and a high initial purchase price, even with a less than stellar current performance on the track, will be claimed as a broodmare. For a breeder, a claim might be a cheaper way to get a quality broodmare than attending the mixed sales auctions as we did.

We took the claiming route without great success. Using a Florida trainer who was tapped into the backside gossip, we dropped claim slips on a number of horses in the winter meet at Gulfstream Park. Not one of the horses we claimed worked out. They included a fast-starting, slow-finishing filly named Line of Fire. We had figured increased stamina was the issue. Unfortunately, once a pop-and-stop horse, many times always a pop-and-stop horse. She was eventually claimed by another conditioner who thought he could do the job we couldn't. (He didn't do it either.) In retrospect, the horse was too close in name to Rapid Fire. (We should have recognized a bad omen when we saw one.) In total, our claiming experience was unrewarding and we vowed not to do it again. The only money we made was with the horse we claimed for $25,000, who was claimed back in the next race for $40,000.

At the same time, Norman was practicing his own brand of claiming at Suffolk Downs and Rockingham Park The game was played just as intently there, but at a much lower price. At the smaller tracks it gets very personal. Trainers who choose not to claim other people's horses usually don't get theirs claimed. In addition, the closeness of the barns makes unsoundness fairly evident. I remember the backside gossip about Cigar when he showed up to run in the Mass Cap at Suffolk. Word was that not many of the wise guy trainers would have claimed him if they had the chance. (Do you detect sour grapes?)

Norman spent his time in New England claiming, getting claimed, and running through the last of our homebreds. He became our most winning trainer in his first year without much purse money to show for his efforts. The cost of ice ate up some of the profit. Trainers at small tracks have a habit of standing their horses in buckets of ice to tighten up their legs and soothe their aches and pains. (For us it was always a major expenditure.)

Evelyn and I showed up at Rockingham Park one Friday night for the evening card. After being wined and dined by Norman and his girlfriend, we watched two of our horses run. They both won, and at the end of the evening, we had two cheap trophies and $4,800 in purse money; but mostly, we felt really good. The winner's circle is the winner's circle, whether it's a stakes race at Belmont or a $4,000 claiming race at Rockingham Park. (The winner's circle is one of the underrated values of the racing game.)

8

Suffolk Downs and Fenway Park

Suffolk Downs, where Norman was plying his trade and we were collecting plastic trophies (actually Suffolk gave little wall plaques, which were quite nice), had become a poster child for small tracks struggling to survive. It is located on the Blue Line of the Massachusetts Transit Authority, a short run from downtown Boston. It's also close to the shore and several waterfront communities. If you looked at it through the eyes of a real estate developer, it had real possibilities. There is plenty of land, good parking, and excellent views.

Buddy Leroux looked at Suffolk Downs through the eyes of a real estate developer, but also the eyes of a Red Sox owner with a plan for developing the land under Fenway Park. If he could build a new stadium for the Sox where Suffolk now stands, he could sell Fenway. The new stadium would attract the huge crowds needed to afford the purchase of big-time players. He was, however, dealing with two venerable land marks. Suffolk Downs was ingrained in the history of thoroughbred racing. It hosted some of the country's greatest racehorses and jockeys. Seabiscuit pounded on the track as did the horses that made the Massachusetts Handicap a legendary race. It also provided jobs, over the years, for many of the well-connected and not so well-connected local people.

Fenway Park was also a true institution. A large part of the history of baseball was written within its walls. Ebbets

Field in Brooklyn, New York, was turned into a housing development when the beloved Dodgers headed for the West Coast, but Fenway and the Red Sox remained. My greatest thrill, as a child, was when my father packed up my brother and me and traveled to Brooklyn from our home on Long Island. We would sit in the right field stands and root for Dixie Walker, who had a liquor store in our hometown. Dixie loved to throw behind runners who turned the wrong way after reaching first base. We cheered for the likes of Pee Wee Reese, Pete Reiser, Duke Snider, Carl Furillo, and their ilk. The same thing was happening between the fans and the players at Fenway. Many of the players stayed there after they retired. One of them, Dom DiMaggio was part of a group bidding against Buddy for the purchase of the franchise. Dom was one of the famous DiMaggio brothers (Joe in New York and Vince in Detroit).

When Buddy's group acquired the team and the park, he began a building campaign that featured the construction of luxury boxes on the roof (the boxes that added such great intrigue to his administration as described earlier). He never changed much of anything else. The Green Monster remained (the close-in left field wall). I brought Evelyn to the park after we built the boxes for him. She wasn't much of a baseball fan and hated all the pre-game commotion on Yawkey Way (the street next to the park). We got in the vintage elevator and Evelyn said, "I hate this." We stepped through an old door onto the roof and she said, "I hate this." I opened the door to the box. She surveyed the carpets, the bar, the sofas, the art and Evelyn said, "Now you're talking." A little bit of neatness in historic Fenway.

Meanwhile at Suffolk Downs, the track was getting a new owner. Buddy had formed a partnership (as he always did) to buy the place. He set up shop with the intention of making a profit. The key to success was the same key required by other tracks around the country—slot machines. They provide not only new customers for pari-mutuel betting, but also a flow of funds to be funneled into purses. Bigger purses, in turn, attract better horses. Better horses mean more customers. A virtuous circle. Many local politicians, however, see no virtue in the addition of slots and fight against them. I've always detected a hint of irony in their position. In search of income for the state's treasury they freely endorse the lottery as a way of raising money. When I was a kid, the lottery was called the numbers racket and the police spent a good deal of their time chasing and busting numbers runners. Now it's perfectly respectable to be selling lottery numbers in local stores throughout the state, without fear of feeding gambling habits. In addition, the money is coming from people who can least afford to be gambling. Some say that the lottery is the most regressive tax of all.

Racetracks, on the other hand, provide surroundings that are already populated by seasoned gamblers. Cash control is also much stronger. The effect of slots on the tracks has proven to be as advertised. States where slots are permitted, have shown a real increase in revenue, and as far as I know, the crime level hasn't shown big increases. (How could it with the amount of checking I was put through as a consequence of my small investment in Suffolk Downs.) In any event, Buddy continued to press a reluctant legislature with threats of imminent closure and loss of jobs. At this writing Massachusetts remains free of the evils of slot machines.

Buddy continued to cling to his hopes right through the negotiations to sell out to a new syndicate, which included my small part. He wrote into the sales agreement an extra payoff for him should slots ever materialize. Meanwhile the new owners set about changing the fortunes of the racetrack. They vowed to bury the name bestowed upon it by frustrated patrons, "Sufferin" Downs.

Norman, with his string of Richlyn Farm horses, was doing his bit to improve the performance of the track. He was buying bags of ice and claiming $4,000 horses like they were going out of style. Shot Gun Evie and Shot Gun Rich were winning an occasional cheap race. Johnny Campo was shipping his worst horses up from Belmont to join in the fun (if you can't make it here, you can't make it anywhere—as the song goes). I hopped on the Blue Line as often as I could to watch our stable in action and Evelyn continued to breed potential Suffolk horses down on the farm. (Talk about your circles.)

The new syndicate did a fairly good job at the Downs. They revived the MassCap and improved the facilities. Good promotions brought in new customers and somewhat better horses started appearing. (We could tell because our horses were winning fewer races.) There was still a profitability problem, however, due to the inability to really turn out big crowds. Over the years, the popularity of off-track betting has cut into racetrack profits. Many of the once important tracks are now wastelands on weekdays, populated by hard-core fans and backside employees. The industry continues to struggle with its image and many states continue to put roadblocks in front of an expanded gaming menu.

9
Racing Overseas

I'm not the vacation type, but as you might expect, Evelyn is. Women really enjoy traveling. The farther and the more expensive, the better. Men are generally content to sit around the house, barbecue, and sleep late. We compromised on trips that allowed us to follow our chosen profession to Ireland, England, and Australia. In fact, our trips to Ireland helped us name several of the progeny of our broodmare, Irish Limerick.

We spent some time in Galway just off the famous bay and close to the track where the Galway jump races are held. We were quite impressed by the toughness of the horses that run in the jumps. One horse, who fell on the second jump, was entered again the next day. When asked why, we were told, "Why not? He didn't finish the race."

In Galway, we found a bar named after Evelyn's family—Killoran. After inquiring about the family, we were directed to a town called Tobercurry on the road to Sligo. Subsequently, the Jockey Club told us that the name Tobercurry was taken so we named our weanling Road to Sligo. (Unfortunately, he never found the road to the winner's circle.) We did, however, find the history of Evelyn's family in Tobercurry. The Killoran restaurant-gift shop-travel agency contained the record of Evelyn's grandmother coming over here after the potato famine (apparently a world changing event for Ireland).

43

We also discovered the following year was a Killoran reunion year, and they were making plans. The plans included designating a Chieftain for the meeting of the clan. The suggestion was made that I would be a fine Chieftain. Evelyn reacted with an indignant, "He can't be the Chieftain. He's German." Apparently, being an American banker was more important than being Irish. (We got the feeling that the reunion was not well-financed.)

Chieftain or not, we returned the next year and we were able to march through town to the cemetery where the local victims of the potato famine were buried. After the parade, all us Killorans retreated to the restaurant and bar where, after eating and drinking, we listened to a speech about the potato famine. On the way back to our motel, we were stopped by several people who said, "I hear that they were discussing the potato famine over at Killoran's tonight" (I guess the Irish remain pretty ticked-off at the English about this issue).

On the way to the Irish Derby, we stopped and climbed the Hill of Slane, inspiring us to name another of Irish Limerick's babies after that tourist site. (Slane's on-track performance was not much better than Sligo's.)

The Derby, that year, was won by an Irish horse, much to the surprise of the local bettors, who didn't seem to be much on providing home team support. While we were there, we visited the National Stud, which features the skeleton of Arkle, the Irish Seabiscuit. Besides reminding us of the potato famine, the skeleton brought back the words of Paddy Riley's ballad, "Arkle, you're the greatest. Arkle, you're the best. You terrorized old England on every racecourse." (It seems that the horse gave Ireland some measure of revenge.)

On the way home, we visited Bunratty Castle, which provided us with a name for another one of Irish Limerick's yearlings. Bunratty Castle has made more than sixty career starts, but won only three times through 2005. (Arkle he's not.) So much for naming horses after the nationality of the mare.

Our vacation trip to England was also quite informative. The same horses travel the circuit to various towns during the season. What's fascinating is they run clockwise at some tracks and counter-clockwise at others. Our experiences trying to get horses to change leads makes me wonder how their animals handle the different directions involved.

Evelyn was particularly impressed by the turned-out lady who visits the saddling paddock before each race and gives an award to the best turned-out horse. Here neatness counts and I'm sure our first trainer (who won Evelyn's neatness award) would have done us proud in England.

We also visited one of the large horse farms where hundreds of acres of grass land are kept groomed by thousands of sheep. Using sheep instead of my Ford tractor and mowing deck would have taken away my best retirement job.

We traveled to Australia for what I hoped was our last international horse vacation. Our destination was the Melbourne Cup. We wanted to see how real men (and women) handled the country's biggest race day. As it turns out, they handle it quite well, but not soberly.

In truth, we never saw so many drunks in one place at the same time, but they were mostly friendly and well-meaning. The horse players don't try to move through the crowds to the betting windows. We met a group of them including a female cop from Queensland who tried to push us out of our three square feet of space by the saddling paddock. When they discovered we were "Yanks" they tolerated our presence, continued to bully other locals, took us into their confidence and shared their booze. We couldn't tell you who won the Melbourne Cup, and we were there.

In any description of our adventures in overseas travel, I would be remiss not to mention our trip to Germany. The trip predated our involvement with horse racing, but it gives you an insight into Evelyn's personality. It happened during my ship lending days. A large New Jersey container ship operation was taking its customers and its bankers to the launching of their newest vessel in a shipyard near Bremen. We all got on a bus and headed for the seashore. Evelyn was sitting right behind the driver, directly under a sign that read "Underhalten mit der Vagonfuherer es Verbotin" (bad German, but it's the best I can remember). The sign didn't stop her from bubbling and chatting with the driver. Someone called out from the back of the bus, "Evelyn, stop under halting." Evelyn didn't and the bus ran into the back of a hay wagon, scattering wagon and hay all over the road. No one was hurt, but forty Americans descended on a small bar near the crash site. Unfortunately, the bar only had thirty glasses, so we drank in shifts. Another good reason for Evelyn to continue her underhalting.

After we had our fill of international travel, we prepared to take on our next important challenge, working with big-time trainers. It was time to remember the old saying—"the best way to make a small fortune in the horse business is to start with a large fortune."

10

Working with Trainers

Since entering the horse business, Evelyn and I had gone through several phases, always learning something as we went. Buying the farm and developing a breeding operation was the first phase. Then we branched out into running our homebreds on the track along with horses claimed from others. Now, we were ready to take the biggest class jump of all, dealing with big-time trainers, buying at big-time auctions, and spending big-time money. As the old saying goes—"If you want to be a big flea, find yourself a big dog." Although we had picked up some fairly good knowledge of the racing business, we were still unprepared for dealing with racing's upper tier. To put it another way—"too soon old, too late smart." (I'm just full of old bromides.) As an aid for others who might want to go in this direction, we have compiled a list of the more common interactions one might have with trainers, and how to make sense of them. (We would have appreciated it if someone had made such a list available to us.)

Trainer Speak

Owners should get a conversion chart with their racing license so they can interpret what the trainers are telling them, and manage them accordingly.

Over the years we have employed a total of eleven trainers from Norman running our homebreds at Suffolk and Rockingham, to big day-rate conditioners at Belmont and Gulfstream with their "don't spare the expense vets and massage specialists."

Despite the apparent differences, these trainers all have something in common. What they tell you must be filtered to get to the truth. The old racetrack adage is—"treat owners like mushrooms—cover them with manure and keep them in the dark." We have learned to listen to "trainer speak" with a slanted ear and found a distinct pattern of words and phrases.

Let's start with the manner in which they deliver bad news. We have found that trainers usually report very bad news in a timely fashion. It generally comes prefaced with words like "I hate to make this call." Nothing good ever comes after these words, just like nothing good ever happens when a boss invites an employee into his office and asks him to close the door. When we hear those dreaded words, I am always tempted to say, "Well, we hate to receive this call." Instead, I just brace myself for the worst.

But unless a disaster has occurred, we have found impending doom is conveyed in stages. One of our trainers liked to start out with something like, "He's a little ouchy." Translation—the horse has a soundness problem that could affect his ability to compete. Another trainer likes the phrase " A little funny behind." Translation—same as above. (Have you noticed the use of "little" in both cases?) When we question these observations, we are usually hit with technical terms. Anatomical phrases pop up such as suspensory, epiglottis, condylar, and we are usually lost after the first few sentences. Vets are more adept at this. Unlike trainers, they never make negative comments, so when we read "racing prognosis guarded" we look for someone who is interested in a riding horse.

To be fair to the trainer, a casual mention of a problem gets the conditioner off the hook should it develop into a bigger problem. The hope, of course, is the situation will clear itself up. (No harm—no foul.)

An excellent time to get a real soundness rundown on your horse is when the trainer proposes a claiming race at a price well below the amount you paid not too long ago. It is then that the little nagging problems, mentioned in passing, take on a bit more reality. In fact one of our trainers once told us our horse runs like a duck (something we missed at the two-year-old in training sale). Head-on shots might be useful in the videos at the sale.

Even before a horse starts racing, the trainer is busy with excuses for the delay in the horse's debut. Many owners see their money being drained away, while the trainer is waiting for the perfect moment to unveil the prodigal child. When we ask when our expensive acquisition might start providing us entertainment at the least and a return on investment at the best, we get answers we have learned to recognize.

"One more work" is a popular line. We had a trainer string us along for quite a while with that. In the same fashion, another would tell us the ideal race was at the end of the month, without mentioning what month. The trainer usually has a reason for the delay. The horse is either too light and needs to put on some weight, or a little "rolly-poly" (a technical term) and needs to take some off. Frustrated with Evelyn's incessant questions, a trainer once told her the horses will tell him when they are ready to run. I suggested we go to the stalls and ask the horses, thereby cutting out the middleman.

I'm sure that you are getting the feeling some trainers wouldn't tell you if your coat was on fire, and that's probably true, but there is one thing an owner can do to level the playing field. Show up with a condition book in hand. (A condition book describes upcoming races at your track by age, sex, distance, and categories.) Better you shouldn't know what races are coming up for your horse, especially when there are other owners' horses with similar conditions looking for similar races. Does the expression about squeaky wheels getting greased come to mind? Start squeaking. (All this could lead to a really noisy barn.)

When the horses start running, new examples of "trainer speak" come to mind. Watching at the track with a trainer at our side, we've heard comments like "she's going the wrong way" (the horse took an early lead and is now being passed). The jockey is not following instructions (hopefully winning the race was part of the instructions). She doesn't like sand in her face—she couldn't get hold of the track, she didn't change leads, all common complaints (she's badly trained is not one we've heard too often).

Many times, you're not at the track. This is more likely with a trainer who runs horses where they can win, even if it costs half the purse to ship him there. In this case, we have found that timing of post-race phone calls varies in direct proportion to the outcome of the race. That is, the better the performance the quicker the call. A victory prompts some trainers to hit the speed dial the second your horse crosses the finish line. If your horse finishes up the track, the phone is usually silent.

Thanks to the internet and extensive television coverage, we usually get the results ourselves. The only thing missing is the post-race dissertation by the trainer. When we finally get the information on a poor performance, it is generally upbeat. My favorite is "the horse came back feeling good and he ate up all his feed." Translation—the horse likes to lose. We were once told our horse was drunk. In fact, when the gates opened, we thought we detected him leaning on the gate wall. Translation—a little too much calming medicine to keep him from acting up in the gate.

Rather than figure all this out for yourself, it might be easier to consult a trainer speak conversion chart with an outline and designations for different reasons (also known as excuses) for a horse's poor performance, delayed debut, or lack of soundness. It could be like that old story about the guy whose jokes were so familiar to everyone he would merely call out a number and everyone would laugh. If nothing else, we would save on phone bills.

11

Ballet Critic

Oblivious of all the movement of horses at Richlyn Farms, Ballet Critic arrived at Belmont Park. The surroundings were completely new to him. He had gotten used to working out on the training tracks in Ocala, but this place was bigger and noisier. Workouts, in the morning, ranged from comfortable gallops to all-out sprints with horses of all ages and sexes coming at him from all angles. Fortunately, he didn't have to deal with the nasty dirt surface when he was working full-out and he avoided having chunks of it thrown into his nose and eyes. The grass training tracks were no great shakes, but genes from a whole bunch of relatives told him that this was a lot better situation for him to be in.

They tried racing him on the dirt occasionally, when the grass track wasn't available, but his efforts seemed to evoke comments like, "He can't stand up on the dirt." Ballet wasn't willing to go that far, however; he understood their attitude.

John Campo seemed to be a pretty good guy. Ballet got the feeling that John was brought up in a horse racing family. His father, apparently, won a race called the Kentucky Derby. He wondered if that race might be in his future. In the meantime, life in the Campo barn was very good. After he won for the first time in July of 2001 he was moved to the place of honor in the stall right next to the boss's office.

From his personal experience and what he gleaned from the other horses, he got the feeling he wasn't being exposed to a lot of expensive medication. Instead, he received, for his minor afflictions, a dose of a secret elixir handed down from father to son (a lot cheaper than Gastrogard or EPM drench). From our conversations with John, both Evelyn and I agreed if he would take the horse home with him at night, he could.

John Campo had his share of interpersonal problems, most trainers do, but he was nothing if not upbeat and confident. He once told a friend of ours about a horse running the next day, "You could ride the horse and he'll win." Our friend didn't ride the horse and he didn't win. (Maybe he should have ridden him.)

Ballet Critic won $71,680 in 2001 with two wins and two seconds out of seven races. His next win was at Delaware in November of 2002. It was one of his few races that we saw in person, although Evelyn had to watch from outside the park gate because they wouldn't let her dog inside. Ballet Critic liked Delaware Park (it's really a pretty track), but he didn't like the idea of their not letting his little buddy in to see him run (he liked Evelyn's West Highland Terrier, Samantha). Filled with confidence from the Delaware race, Campo entered him in a stakes race at Aqueduct, a race he darn near won. He led to the middle of the stretch but faded to seventh, just three lengths off the winner.

About that time, Ballet Critic was featured in the *Belmont Post Parade* magazine under the headline—"What's not to like? Ballet Critic runs hard at big prices." In the article, Campo was quoted as saying, "He's an honest horse, who gives you all he's got." If Ballet could read, he would have loved the quote and probably replied, "John also gives me all he's got."

Ballet won again, at Colonial Downs in the summer of 2003 and went on to his winter home in Pennsylvania. John exited the horse racing business in early 2004 and we had to find a new conditioner. Campo's final record with Ballet was twenty-five races—four wins, three seconds, one third, and $144,400 in purse money.

It turned out to be quite easy to place our horse. Ballet just loved his winter home, and why shouldn't he? Bernie Houghton and his family have a very nice farm. Acres of fields surrounding modern barns with up-to-date equipment. Most of all, Ballet liked the people, and they loved him. We decided to let Bernie run the horse off his farm at the mid-Atlantic tracks.

Slate Ledge Pride would have loved the farm as well. For exercise, Bernie would let Ballet run up and down the grassy fields, some belonging to his neighbors. One day Ballet was charging down a slope right at a group of sheep who had just been let out on to his course. Without missing a step, he dodged and weaved through the herd like a football running back. The thought of shying away or pulling up never entered his mind. He would have been perfectly content at the farm in England and its grass-eating sheep.

Another favorite of Ballet was the point-to-point races. Local gentleman farmers would gather on the weekends and run a designated course on the grass fields. Jockeys, mostly jump people, wear their colors and race for trophies and pride. As exercise, Bernie let Ballet Critic participate. The last win picture he produced from his efforts showed a jockey easily the size of the football running back we discussed earlier. Ballet is a big horse, but in the win picture he looked like a pony. I suspect, when Slate told Ballet Critic about the little people he had toted around, he never anticipated the size of the guy his protege lugged across the finish line in the picturesque fields of Pennsylvania.

The 2004 racing season was a particularly wet one as evidenced by the lack of grass racing at Saratoga Springs that summer. As a result Ballet Critic had an easy year, only three races and no checks of any consequence. In 2005 he was back in the game, with one win, four seconds and a third, not bad for a seven-year-old.

Between races, which were coming rather frequently due to the lack of rain, Ballet was left to "hack around" in the woods. He didn't mind, because the training track had become boring absent the heat of competition. To him, hacking around meant new sights and sounds. He jumped an occasional fence, probably looking to pick up a new skill that might prove useful after he retires from the big track. We think he might also have a future siring show horses for the area. (We're not telling him because he might feign injury and speed up his retirement date.)

Having Bernie and his farm sitting in Pennsylvania has helped us to discourage our big-time trainers from shipping to Philadelphia or Delaware (at great expense) to win an easier race. My line is, "If the horse can't win in the New York circuit, Bernie will be happy to pick him up and run him off the farm." (Ballet Critic can use the company, someone to hack around in the woods with.)

12

Choosing a Trainer

Our years in the horse business began to accumulate. We believed the racing side is where we wanted to stay. The broodmare farm had been fun, good, honest work, multiple challenges, but in the end, just too frustrating. Since leaving the breeding side, we had wandered from trainer to trainer, without a real plan. The experience did teach us what to watch for and how to understand the trainer's thought process. It had also showed us how to lose money. Our goals fluctuated from having plenty of races to watch (entertainment), to owning well-known horses (prestige), to actually making money. After discarding the latter as unattainable, we concentrated on reaching the first two goals.

The most important decision to be made was selecting a trainer. As with most married couples, our personal likes and dislikes came into play. Evelyn was leaning toward the big-time trainers with the prestigious client list, while I preferred the old-time trainers struggling to keep their clients happy by keeping their costs down (always the money grubbing banker).

A problem with the most popular trainers was the number of animals under their control. Where I preferred the big fish in a little pond philosophy, Evelyn was willing to flap her flippers with the other big fish and hope some of their class rubbed off. It is a problem, however, when a trainer has

56

multiple candidates in his barn for each race and has to choose among a bunch of anxious owners. I'm sure Evelyn was counting on her personal charm to win the day. Since I have no charm at all, I need to be the only choice a trainer has for a particular race. There is also the amount of customer shmoozing a trainer with a large barn can do. Many of the more popular conditioners have turned to electronic assistance for their public relations. Some have developed web sites where owners can log on to find out their expensive purchases are not scheduled to run, and indeed, have not even worked out recently. Others fax daily or weekly reports on the progress or lack of progress their horses are making.

My kind of trainer makes it more of an adventure to find out how our horses are progressing. We can go to the barn frequently to check each horse out for obvious physical problems, or we can carefully analyze the vet bills to uncover some unreported malady. Another favorite activity of mine is grilling grooms and exercise riders about the racing readiness of our animals. Since many trainers caution their people about talking to owners, it takes all my acting skills to obtain information. As I have pointed out many times to Evelyn, my approach adds mystery and intrigue to the business of owning racehorses. (She, of course, thinks I'm full of cold tea.)

There is something to be said, however, for being one of the trainer's major owners. To attain that position, care and feeding of your conditioner is important. The competition for owners who pay their bills in a timely manner is fierce, and if you refrain from telling the trainer how to do his job, you might be in demand. We always pay our bills on the day we receive them, figuring if you intend to pay them eventually, you might as well get points for paying promptly. As far as telling them how to do their job, I always preferred to have the trainer take the blame for a bad decision. If he listens to you, he can always wash his hands of a poor outcome. It's the same with buying horses. Let the conditioner choose the horses he is going to condition. Then, you can do future whining in good conscience if the purchases turn out to be duds. Our overall philosophy has always been, if you don't like the way a trainer trains, get a new one.

It's good to avoid moving from barn to barn, so making an informed decision early on is important. If the trainer knows you are not wedded to his operation, that's usually enough to get a fair share of attention. Of course, Evelyn's desire to have a popular trainer reduces your leverage quite a bit, because the trainer usually has plenty of well-heeled clients on his waiting list. My trainer choice can ill afford to lose a paying client, especially one who pays on time.

The personality and appearance of the trainer are also a consideration. Evelyn seems to prefer men (and good-looking ones at that). I have a different set of preferences. In fact, one of the things that attracted me to Johnny Campo early on was how much he reminded me of Buddy Leroux. Not only his appearance, but also the look in his eye which challenged you to think one step ahead of him or pay the price. (I've always loved a challenge and I have come to appreciate a good line of baloney when I hear one.)

One decision we did make, now that our farm in Ocala was no longer turning out cheap runners, was to move up the food chain in horse quality and give our trainers better, more expensive stock. That worked well with Evelyn's plan, because big-time trainers prefer to work with big-time horses. It's the same virtuous circle we discussed previously. Expensive horses with their top-class pedigrees and outstanding conformation are more likely to win races. More wins mean people give the trainers more quality horses, which improves the trainers' win percentage. The same circle works for the best jockeys whose agents get the best horses from the best trainers and therefore the jockey's wins continue to roll in.

In addition to a primary trainer, it's also smart to keep horses with more than one conditioner. Not only is competition healthy, but also certain training styles fit certain horses. Location helps as well. Our man Bernie on the farm in Pennsylvania provides access to the mid-Atlantic tracks with their somewhat easier races. Ballet Critic appreciated that as he appreciated the bucolic surroundings on the farm. Many trainers head south for the winter, while others prefer to stay in the northeast to take advantage of the statebred conditions for some of their horses and the reduction in day-to-day competition. Grass horses have to go south or be laid up, but many horses with good mud pedigrees thrive on the winter conditions up north.

Horses with more moderate ability are more profitably run by more frugal trainers with lower day rates. It's nice to have the ability to move a horse down the cost ladder, while making room for more expensive horses with the more expensive trainers. Matching the cost of running a horse with the level of purses available is always a smart move. By having several trainers, you can move individual horses without moving the whole string.

After we settled on our trainers for the long haul, and Evelyn mostly got her way, I started to work on a strategy that would spread what money we had over a maximum number of years. Without formally checking a mortality table, I figured that we would reach a point where we wouldn't care how our horses are doing and we planned to run out of money at about that time. With our last coins, we would call our children to come and pick us up. (The kids really loved this plan.)

Actually, what we did was put their inheritance in a trust for each of them. They control it and get it in ten years. We planned to lose everything else in the horse business, although the son who named his first born after me and pointed his daughter into the hunter-jumper sport is making points. (I'm easily conned.)

13
Controlling Your Trainer

Our travels through the horse business have brought us to our present stop, the big-time trainer The air up there is quite rarified because of the money involved. This is not a place for owners of little courage or little financial support. We had been losing money steadily since we began this trip back in the days of Buddy Leroux, mountainside horse farms, and the Red Sox. Now we faced the prospect of losing at an even faster rate or (gasp) making the big score. Plastic trophies at Rockingham Park will no longer do the job.

As I mentioned in trainer speak, different trainers have different approaches to spending your money in search of the holy grail of racing, a horse capable of making big bucks. Take medication as an example. As Ballet Critic pointed out, some trainers will avoid expensive medicine and opt for homemade remedies (the chicken soup approach to conditioning). Others believe every dollar (of your money) spent to give your horse even a slight advantage on the track is money well spent. Although they are quick to point out their expenditures will not make an untalented animal into a talented one, they seem to give the same treatment to every horse in their barn, prince and pauper alike.

After musing over the vet bill from one of our big-time trainers, I considered the value of electric therapy, injecting joints for lubrication, Gastrogard with no sign of ulcers, EPM drench with no sign of EPM, and wondered why our other trainer's vet bill that month was only $75. I asked him and he said, "Why not? The horse wasn't sick." I didn't remember any difference in the performance of the two trainers. (It does make one think.)

Another area of divergence between trainers is how they handle shipping. Certain shipping requirements are built-in. Moving between parts of the country when seasons change is one example, another is moving between the barn and the track when the conditioner is not able to have stalls within walking distance. The real incremental van expense comes from trainers whose basic philosophy is, "I run my horses where they can win" (no matter how far away they have to go). Other trainers believe in the home-court advantage and never stray from familiar surroundings and familiar jockeys who know the track and the horse.

Differences also exist between trainers in the type of transport they use. The choices range from box stalls with all the creature comforts to crowding in a van with a bunch of horses going in the same direction. Ballet Critic, a sociable kind of guy, always indicated that he preferred the latter. Chatting with other horses helps to pass the time. Besides, you can learn a lot about the track you are going to and the horses you are going to run against. If Ballet had the opportunity to talk to the Maryland-bound horses heading with him to a stakes race, he might have learned something. He would, at least, have been able to endorse John Campo's comment after the race, "If you put a Maryland jockey on your horse, expect a Maryland ride."

Another way a trainer can eat into your life savings is by displaying all sorts of confidence in your horses and nominating them for every stakes race available, no matter how remote their participation might be. I recall being encouraged to pay installments on a Florida Stallion Stakes race long before our colt was ready. As the race date approached, I was told to check-in before we made any more payments (not a great sign). A good way to follow up on this issue is to carefully examine your horseman's account. If we ran in and won every stakes race we were nominated for (and charged for), Evelyn would have gotten the owner of the year award.

There is hope, however. A middle ground can be reached between trainer extremes. The frugal, stay-at-home trainer, without impossible dreams of stakes winning success can be encouraged to spend a little more of your money on vet bills, and travel to nearby tracks, occasionally, to pick up an easy win. The difficult task is to rein in the spending habits and the glorious visions of the conditioner on the other extreme. These tendencies have their roots in dealing with people who have an endless supply of money. They are the "if you have to ask how much it costs, you can't afford it" crowd. Your conditioner might have a bunch of owners of this type already, or he may have learned the trade from a trainer who specializes in that stratum of wealth. We have discovered the latter provides a more fertile ground for change than the former. In the final analysis, moving to another barn might be the only practical solution.

My years in corporate America, before the racing bug bit me, taught a basic lesson in handling people who work for you. (Lest you forget, trainers do work for you.) The lesson is—If you can set up a situation where your subordinates' goals are the same as yours, any results are easier to obtain. In other words, your trainer must see your total day-to-day costs as the trainer's costs and they impact directly on the success of the bottom line. A conditioner can't measure your expenses only in the context of the day rate. They must include van bills, vet bills, and entry fees as well. The trainer must understand if it takes two years to earn back the purchase price of your horse, the money you spent on it over the same time period must be considered. (Trainers will say of course they know that, but they really don't.)

I like to call this approach the report card, and it isn't easy to sell. Certainly the old-time trainer, or the offspring of old-time trainers, won't touch it with a ten-foot pole (Campo tried to throw me out of his office), but they tend to fall on the frugal side of the equation anyway.

The plan is simple, but it must be tied to an incentive to make it work. The incentive would be your annual expenditure for new horses. We set a dollar limit on the amount we budget for sale purchases each year and promise to spend the money. The trainer picks out the animals and knows his success is bound up in the quality of those purchases. Although a profitable, well-publicized runner is the goal of every owner, it is even more important to the trainer, whose future client base is on the line.

Once you have agreed on a purchase amount for next year's purchases of yearlings or two-year-olds in training, the expense calculation kicks in. On a horse-by-horse basis you total up all the expenses and match that total against the net purse revenue. Each month you arrive at a net profit or loss figure. The result of the calculation is either added to or subtracted from the amount budgeted for the sales.

The result of all these mental gymnastics is that the trainer sees, very clearly, overspending without a corresponding increase in purse revenue can rapidly deplete the new horse pipeline to which he attaches his future success. In our case, it has led to less unnecessary shipping, lower vet bills, and more judicious nominations. Remember, however, you can adjust behavior, but you can't really change it.

The important role of the owner is not to exceed the derived spending cap at the sales, and to live up to your spending commitment each year.

64

Controlling trainers at the auctions is also important as you will see in the next chapter, which again highlights the differences among them.

14

Sales and Syndicates

At this writing, the results of Day Two of the Keeneland yearling sale catch my eye. Sheikh Mohammed bin Rashid at Maktoum has just bought a colt for $9.7 million. In addition to pointing out where all the real money in the world is, it opens the ongoing question of how much you should spend on a horse. It always makes me smile to watch everyone congratulate a successful bidder at an auction. Since it doesn't take much skill to pay the most for a horse under heavy bidding, I guess they are congratulating the Sheikh for having the most money. (I join them in the accolade—I wish we had that much.)

When studies are done tracing the long-term earnings of multimillion-dollar purchases, including eventual sale as a sire, the results seem to point to them as bad buys. On the other hand, a quick review of the horses winning the Kentucky Derby in recent years shows remarkably low-priced horses getting the trophy.

It makes common sense that higher-priced horses with better pedigrees and more appealing confirmations will succeed at a better than average rate. The real questions are: How much better? And at what additional price? Since the percentage of success out of any given number of purchases tends to be rather low (successes as measured by being in the black); buying a lager number of cheaper horses might be an alternative to one expensive buy. On the other hand, the high daily expense level of the big-time trainer could favor a small number of high-priced animals. It costs the Sheikh the same amount each month to support his $9.7 million horse as it did for us to provide bed and board for Rapid Fire.

It seems the decision on purchase price is a tough one, but many times the trainer makes it for you. Some will refuse to overpay for a horse who may not recover its costs, while others believe each of his purchases is the next Derby winner and "if we miss this opportunity, we will regret it forever."

With these conflicting pressures in mind, this might be a good point to describe the auction process and our experience with it.

We participate in most of the big auctions of young horses each year. They include the Fasig-Tipton Saratoga yearling sale, the Keeneland yearling sale, and the Ocala two-year-old sale at Calder Racetrack. They are preceded by catalogues designed to provide sufficient pedigree and performance information to help buyers decide which animals they wish to examine in person. Each consignor sets up shop in a discreet area and provides browsers with a variety of pens, refreshment, and smiling horsewalkers. They keep a careful record of the showings to get a feel for the popularity of each horse. This is useful information when determining a reserve price, if one is utilized. (In theory, the higher the interest level, the more lively the bidding.)

Due to the large number of horses consigned to the auction, most buyers compile a viewing list from the catalogues, while a few, more ambitious, buyers will look at every horse in the sale first and then read the catalogue. Lookers at the horse auctions always remind me of home buyers who try not to show much enthusiasm for the house they are looking at, even if they love it, in order to help in the price negotiation. Although negotiation is not part of the auction process, the consignor has the ability to re-set the reserve price at the last moment in order to set up artificial competition for the buyer who has fallen in love with the horse.

The reserve system is artificial if there is no bidding between two buyers. The auctioneer cleverly works the reserve into the exchange and since all the bidders may not be in the room (some are on the phone and are in the back of the arena), it's hard to detect. The hammer price is the final bid and if it's above the reserve level, the horse is sold. If not, the horse is an RNA (reserve not attained), and returned to the seller. Consignor and auction company commissions are based on the hammer price and are paid by the seller, even though the horse is taken back.

The old hands know who the big buyers are at every sale. In the case of the Sheikh, even the new hands were aware of him. Big buyers are watched wherever they go and some people piggyback on their interest, thereby upping the potential sales price. As a result, the poker face of the big buyer can reach extreme levels. We had a trainer who was so wary of this issue he would apparently turn down a yearling as it exited the stall, though he may have just seen what he considers the best horse in the sale.

This approach often carries over to the bidding. Wayne Lukas has this cute little thing he does with his finger on the side of his nose (sort of like Santa Claus) to protect his bid, rather than give away his interest in the animal being auctioned. The spotters (people who elicit bids in different areas of the arena and pass them up to the podium) are aware of the little tricks of the big buyers and watch for them.

In our first auction, we were not burdened by having a lot of money to bid with, or anyone who would have had the slightest interest in what we were doing. Evelyn showed no subtleties at all when bidding. She waved her arms and made sure the spotter saw her.

Even the more sophisticated buyers have difficulty following the bids. If the podium has received a bid at $50,000 they start calling $55,000 so quickly the first bidder isn't sure if the $50,000 is his and sometimes bids again at the new level. Since many of the bidders are unseen or part of the reserve process, it's easy (and expensive) to make such a mistake.

Our approach is to sit near a spotter who will keep us personally aware of where our bid stands. He'll say, "It's you—it's you," until a new bid arrives. Then he'll say, "Okay, now you can bid." (Not very sophisticated, but it works for us.)

Just as trainers differ in their approach to conditioning, they also differ in the way they buy horses. You don't have to use a trainer at the auction. An experienced agent will accommodate you for a fee. The trainer, however, has a long-term interest in running the horse and improving his own reputation as a conditioner. There is usually no fee involved. It also gives the owner the right to whine about the poor performance of one of the purchased horses without having to hear Johnny Campo's favorite line—"I do the best I can with the stock I got."

Frugal conditioners are also frugal buyers, while ebullient trainers buy with the same panache. Knowing this, we try to attend the auctions when we can and follow them closely by phone and computer when we can't. The frugal trainer has a purchase price in mind and is prepared to move on to another horse when the bidding exceeds that level. As the future owners, we usually fall in love with one of the horses and when the trainer reaches the pre-set level, we prod and push for the trainer to spend more of our money. The ebullient trainer has fallen in love as well and tries to prod us past our pre-set limit. I remember a sale where our limit was $200,000. When the bidding passed that level, I lost interest and began to check the catalogue for our next horse of interest. Suddenly, our favorite spotter was in my face saying, "The bid is $285,000. I guarantee the horse is yours for $290,000." Startled, I turned to my trainer, who flashed me a sheepish grin, and my wife, who was saying, "Go ahead and bid again. My husband is such a cheapskate."

This is where the report card approach is quite useful. No matter how much the trainer likes the horse, the finite amount of money available must be considered. If it all goes on one horse, there is nothing left for another purchase. The question of one expensive horse rather than two less expensive ones is now in play.

There is also the decision of which, and how many, sales to go to. If the money available for two-year-olds is all used up in the fall yearling sales, there is no need to attend the spring two-year-old sales. One trainer came up with the possibility of buying an RNA from the Saratoga yearling sale. My response was, "Fine, if you would rather have this horse than one you might find in the Keeneland yearling sale, be my guest." (He decided to go to Keeneland.) That was more support for my personal policy of getting everybody singing out of the same songbook.

Following a sale on my computer gives me a lot less control, especially with the ebullient trainer. After checking out all the horses, I would get a list of the most-favored hip numbers. I would refer to the pedigree pages, hoping for weak families. Strong pedigrees would mean expensive prices, while a weaker background would make them affordable. We were faced with that situation one day, a horse with a modest stud fee and a yearling price of $11,000 was selling in a two-year-old sale. The trainer loved him and I was feeling good about our chances of getting him. Evelyn was not quite as happy. "I don't want to be seen buying a cheap horse," she said. When the hammer came down, Evelyn got her way. We paid $250,000 for this seemingly bargain horse.

Then there is the business of pinhooking. The people who bought our horse for $11,000 and sold him for $250,000 made a profit, before fees, of $239,000. It reflects the degree to which a horse can improve in a short period of time and the bidding power of several well-financed buyers who settle on the same animal. They paid more attention to his athleticism than his pedigree. Pinhookers try to keep their purchase price low enough so they can profit on the resale. Bidding against them when you plan to race the horse usually works to your advantage because they are likely to stop bidding before you do. They also look for early foals who can be made ready in time to run well in the under tack show. In addition, they look for hot sires who have a chance of getting hotter before the two-year-old sale.

Pinhooking is always a possibility for us even though we are concentrating on racing. If one of our yearlings looks commercially feasible by the time the two-year-old sale arrives, there is always the option of selling it. If the right price isn't offered, we could race him as planned. A pitfall might be Evelyn's habit of falling in love with her horses. Pinhooking would require keeping the horse away from her until after the sale. This problem also exists with claiming races, into which many of Evelyn's favorite horses have disappeared over the years. A side benefit, especially with the ebullient trainers, would be to use the pinhooking approach to keep their high-priced purchase tendencies in check. The cheaper horses we buy and can't sell could lower the average cost of our stable.

As you can see, we have not yet decided whether we should have a few expensive horses or many cheaper ones. It may be a cowardly way out, but I guess we've settled on dealing with several trainers, each with a different approach, and letting the chips fall where they may.

If all of the above seems hard to deal with, there is an alternative—syndication. It gives the prospective owner the ability to let others deal with the trainer. Syndicates like Centennial Farms, West Point Thoroughbreds, and Dogwood Stable have introduced many new participants to thoroughbred racing. I recall having lunch, back in my banker days, with Don Little of Centennial Farms. It was his pitch, at the time, for me to introduce his program to our trust and investment customers as a great place to invest their funds. Even as a horse-loving banker, I couldn't bring myself to endorse racing as a good investment.

Even if it's not a prudent home for your savings, syndication remains a good way to enjoy the fun of horseracing at an affordable price. The problem of dealing with a trainer is replaced with the issue of dealing with the partners. The trainer has a much bigger public relations problem than he, in many cases, is used to.

One of our trainers, Pat Kelly, tried syndication with a group of owners. Pat is a solid trainer with a long pedigree in the business. His father, Tom Kelly, is in the Hall of Fame and still makes the scene in the barn area.

You can tell a syndicate is involved when you see a crowd of people surrounding a horse in a saddling ring. Ditto for the winner's circle. The same crowd shows up in the morning to watch their horse work out. I recall being at Kelly's barn one morning, chatting with some of the syndicate members. I inquired as to how they were getting along and was told they were all on the same page. To test their conviction, as their horse galloped by, I said, "I'll buy that horse for $100,000." About half of them said, "We'll take it," and the other half said, "Not on your life." (Good luck to them in the future.)

15

New Trainer and New Horses

At the February Ocala Breeders' Sales Co. two-year-old sale at Calder racetrack, hip number 35, consigned by Tony Bowling and Bobby Dodd, was a Valid Expectations colt out of a Grub mare named Grub's Dancer. The stallion was relatively new without any notable progeny, and the mare showed little in the way of performance on the track.

The colt caught George Weaver's eye as he patiently reviewed the tapes of the under tack show. He watched every horse work and filtered out the ones with questions about the way they moved. Traveling quickly from barn to barn, he brought out each horse and watched them walk the well-worn path.

George has long legs and he moves fast. I know, because I was trying to keep up with him. My recent hip operation slowed me down some and by the time I got to hip 35, he was already out of his stall.

We had just taken on George as a trainer and this was his first chance to pick out horses for us. In fact, this was the first opportunity he had to purchase a horse for anyone. He and his wife Cindy had just left the Todd Pletcher barn to start their own operation. They had initially transferred with Pletcher from the Wayne Lukas barn.

Our first contact with Weaver arose from a casual meeting Evelyn had at the Saratoga Springs YMCA. One of Pletcher's exercise riders, named Willie, overheard her talking horses, interrupted, and suggested he try this new kid, who just went out on his own. Willie persisted with his sales job over the next month, even showing up in the saddling paddock while John Campo was tacking up one of our horses. John peered out from under the horse wondering who this little pitchman was. (He could ill-afford to lose a client.) Finally succumbing to Willie's enthusiasm, Evelyn invited George over to our house in Florida, and the relationship built from there.

The first milestone was the two-year-old sale where we tasked him to buy us three horses in the $100,000 range. For us, it was a fairly big step. Just four years ago we would have been buying four horses for the price of one of these.

It's Weaver's style to select the best looking, most athletic horses in the sale, and if the pedigree is also good, we would be talking big bucks. In the case of hip 35, we seemed to be in luck. The pedigree didn't exactly shout "buy me." Maybe he wasn't going to attract a lot of lookers. He was, however, an attractive animal.

Hip 35 looked us over as well. He had one wild eye, which we always thought displayed intelligence in a horse and, in this case, a good deal of mischief. To him, we looked like a tall young fellow (George is only thirty-four) and an old guy with a limp. We seemed to be pleasant enough, and just might be the right people to take him into the next phase of his career. He also hoped there would be some females in our group, because he really did like them the best. He also wondered what the procedure was for going from here to where this group or any other of the assorted lookers were.

Hip 35 found out. He was walked from his stall to the saddling paddock (quite a distance at Calder), and then brought into the sales ring. He was surrounded by people and overseen by a guy on a podium, wielding a mean looking hammer. At this sale, the setup is very cozy, and hip 35 could cast his wild eye around the crowd. He studied the assembled buyers and noted the bid spotters, who seemed to enjoy whooping it up and jumping around.

I sat next to Weaver, mostly to contain his enthusiasm, which gets fairly high when he's bidding on a horse he really, really likes. My goal was to hold him in the $100,000 range. It occurred to me it might be possible with hip 35. I remembered our experience with his mare's sire, Grub, down in Ocala. The farm standing him had all sorts of problems getting his mares in foal, even to the point where they contemplated breeding him in the field. Consequently, the stud fee wasn't much.

Hip 35's spirits picked up when he saw who was bidding on him. The tall guy was in there, and best of all, a cute little woman seemed to be part of the group. He wasn't sure when the hammer went down (that annoying hammer), who bought him. He suspected it was the right people when he saw a woman with a clip board heading in their direction.

We finished the day with three new horses. In addition to hip 35, we purchased a Runaway Groom colt (turned out to be slightly unbalanced—could run ok, but couldn't walk—was eventually claimed for $15,000 after winning one race), and a big, tough looking colt by Grand Slam (body grew faster than his legs—won one race—Bernie sold him for $7,500 off the farm to a gentleman farmer). Each of the horses cost exactly $100,000. George Weaver always said if you get one good horse out of every three you buy, you are doing well. In this case, a point well taken.

We visited the barns after the sale to see where our hard-earned money had gone. At this point you hope to avoid coming down with a case of buyer's remorse.

Hip 35 saw us coming, and breathed a sigh of relief. The right people bought him, and that cute little lady is still aboard. When we asked to see our new horse, the reply was,

"Great—you bought Calvin." "Calvin?" we replied and discovered we had bought the class clown. Apparently, his wild eye did indicate mischief as we had suspected. As he came out of his stall, we were reminded of Evelyn's puppy who was always trying to grab his leash out of your hands.

I asked Weaver to pick which of our three purchases he liked the best. I wanted to give him my best available name. He picked hip 35 and Saratoga County officially entered our life.

16

The Big Horse Arrives

After the high of the auction sales (spending a lot of money in a short period of time has an opiate effect), both the trainer and the owners suffer a bit of a let-down. For the owner it's suddenly realizing how he could have better employed his funds, for the trainer, it's "what did I see in these horses, and can I really get my owner's money back." As the new horses paraded down the ramp to the Weaver barn, all the little imperfections appeared to get larger. George watched Cindy's face as the horses arrived. She is really the definitive judge of how her husband did at the sale. In many cases, she has to retrain them and watch closely as all the stuff the consignor has pumped into them to improve their performance starts to wear off.

Watching the latest shipment, Cindy noted that the Grand Slam colt was a little out of proportion and would need to do some growing. The Runaway Groom needed to get his head together. The Valid Expectations colt, however, seemed to have it right.

Hip 35 sees the same thing in Cindy. The tall guy's heart seems to be in the right place and the owners look OK (especially the woman), but this female is looking right into his soul.

After a period of R&R, to recover from the sale, the horses are now at Palm Meadows in South Florida, preparing for the spring and summer campaign that will kick off their racing careers. Saratoga County loves his stall. It's brand new as is the whole facility, recently built by Frank Stronach as part of his grand design for Florida. The barns are big and airy and the track is comfortable.

First on Saratoga's agenda is to collect some toys and find people to play with (they didn't call him Calvin for nothing). He used his proven method for attracting attention—he bit people. Not a nasty bite, mind you, but a grab for loose articles of clothing. His style was unique. He would set up shop toward the back of the stall until they leaned in to see him and dart forward with his head at an angle for maximum biting flexibility. With his long neck, he usually hit his target. Our first encounter had me jumping back and pulling in my midsection. Saratoga got me anyway as he did most people, leaving a purple pinch mark in his wake. (Evelyn and I compared purple marks that evening.)

For Saratoga County, it was mission accomplished. His early biting tactics earned him an orange highway cone which stood in front of his stall to warn people passing by. He also was given a rubber ball, hung on a string, on which he could vent his chewing energies. He really liked the cone. Saratoga discovered by grabbing the narrow top, he was able to swing it back and forth, get some real momentum and fling it pretty far.

George and Cindy tolerated his behavior, because it was all mischief without malice. It didn't really bother them until the day he grabbed their young son, Benjamin, by the back of his coat with the intention of launching him in the air to see if he could best the distance record of the traffic cone.

The female exercise riders took to him right away and he to them. Heather, a tough, experienced rider, loved to get in his stall and battle him head-to-head. Knocking people around and being knocked by them was one of his best things. Allison, who became his regular rider, was Saratoga's favorite right from the beginning.

In his young life, Saratoga County had plenty of people on his back. Like Slate Ledge Pride and Ballet Critic, he learned to handle their peculiarities. He was always in charge. He ran when he wanted to run and rested when he wanted to rest. Allison understood him and their friendship, which started at Palm Meadows in South Florida, eventually spread halfway around the world to Dubai in the United Arab Emirates.

Saratoga County got right into the exercise routine. He understood what everyone wanted. He was to go out every morning and either jog, or gallop, or breeze (they called it a breeze, but it seemed like hard work). When the exercise was over, he could go back to his stall and grab forty winks. Not many horses ever learn to relax. He mastered it.

Another good part of the morning workouts was the number of equine friends he made. He was usually working with another horse from the Weaver barn. They would chat going down the backstretch, commenting on the weather and how much better looking the exercise riders were in Florida. If asked for more effort, Saratoga would, grudgingly, pick up the pace. Neither horse would try to outdo or embarrass the other. (What did these riders know anyway?) Leaving the track the two horses would congratulate each other for getting away with a minimum of effort.

None of this went unnoticed by George and Cindy, who worried that this big, muscular animal lacked competitive instincts. Some horses, especially those as affable as Saratoga County, never really get into racing, or figure out how important working hard and succeeding is (I know people like that). They have one thing in common. They are happy.

In the late spring, the Weaver barn packed up and headed for Saratoga Springs, New York, where our favorite horse was to come face-to-face with the place he was named for. He had not changed his style. He was as affable as ever. The rubber ball came with him as did his battered highway cone. He also had picked up a new trick. When given a plastic Coke bottle full of water, he would grab it by the neck, tilt it back, and drink from it. However, none of this was making us any money.

In an attempt to get Saratoga County down to business, George stopped running him with his friends and stable-mates. It didn't work, because he quickly made new friends when he got to the track. (For Saratoga County, life was all about love at first sight.) The meet opened and we (as owners usually do) started whining about when our horses were going to run their first race. We were especially strident about Saratoga County, who looked to be healthy, robust, and ready to go. George Weaver, at that point, wasn't sure what he wanted to do. He settled for a $75,000 maiden claimer at five and one half furlongs on Saturday, August 28, 2003. A day we will never forget.

George had held off Saratoga's first race until almost the end of the meet, while his sales mates were running but not producing much. Evelyn argued against the claiming part. We had paid $100,000 for the animal and now he was being offered to the public for 75 percent of the price. The town was filled with trainers and owners who attended the Fasig-Tipton sales and were willing to pay ten times that amount for unproven yearlings, who didn't even look as good as our horse.

As I mentioned earlier, this is the point where the trainer gives you a detailed description of every blemish, real or imagined. "If he's claimed, especially for $75,000, it may not be a bad thing" is the line they would use. George took a different approach. He explained, "The horse is lazy, without a competitive attitude or a killer instinct. Losing would only make it worse. Let's put him in where he has a chance to win first time out, and anyway, trainers would be afraid there was something wrong with a $100,000 horse being offered for $75,000 without ever having raced." (I guess that was reverse psychology.)

The rest is, as they say, history. With John Velazquez aboard, Saratoga County broke last, was bumped around, but managed to rejoin the pack after the first quarter-mile. He seemed to be watching the other horses with his wild eye and instantly understanding what he had to do. (Or was it he found no friends to run with.) In any event, he burst through at the half-mile marker and left the field in the proverbial cloud of dust, finishing almost ten lengths ahead of the place horse.

George leaped from his seat next to us and disappeared in the same proverbial cloud of dust, on his way to the winner's circle. We followed with a mixture of happiness and apprehension. A winded George Weaver met us in the circle with three words, "He wasn't claimed." (In the end, those words were worth about $1 million each.)

In the months to come, Saratoga's maiden win was to elicit a good deal of comment. There were congratulations and questions about our sanity for running the horse for $75,000. (Monday morning quarterbacks.) The most interesting came from Johnny Campo. He indicated that he had inquiries from several trainers before the race as to why "your people" were running their $100,000 horse for $75,000. His answer, according to John, was, "If you claim that horse, I'll kick your butt."

Saratoga County returned to his stall that evening not knowing Campo may have saved him from losing "his people," but content with the knowledge he can run hard when he wants to. He suspected it all long, but it was nice to prove it to himself. Now maybe he can get some rest and go back to being affable in the morning.

The Adventure Begins

The Dude Rancher

Slate Ledge Pride

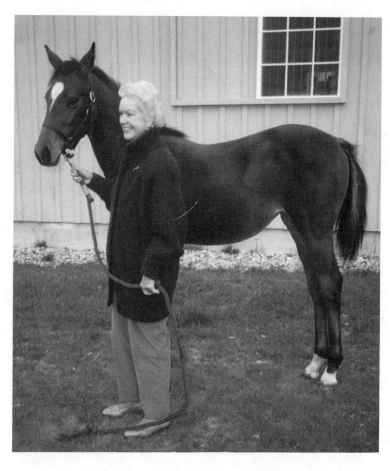

Jen's True Heart—Our Foundation Mare

Shot Gun Evie Wins Our First Race

Finding Evelyn's Irish Roots

Evelyn at the Melbourne Cup

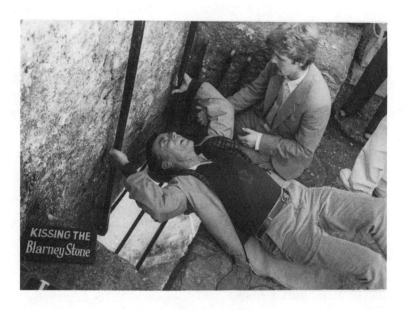

An Author in Training

Trainer Speak

Ballet Critic

Looking Up to Your Jockey

Ballet Carries a Heavy Load

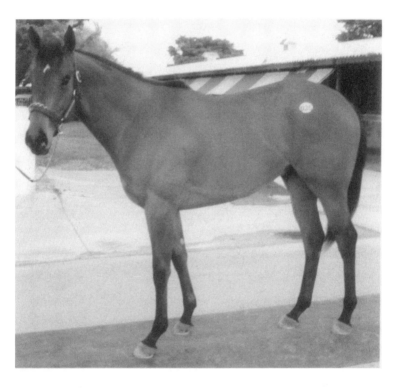

Saratoga County—Hip Number 35

With Allison in Kentucky

Saratoga County Wins the Big One

George and Javier in Dubai

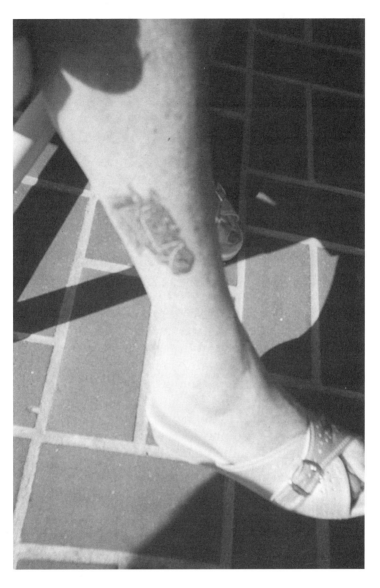

Evelyn's Tattoo from the Dubai Win

17

Early Success

Saratoga County's maiden race was our first win at Saratoga Springs, and to date, our only win. It's a tough place to race, especially two-year-olds. The meet comes fairly early in their racing careers, and only the earliest foals and the more mature horses have a real chance. The biggest of the big-time trainers who have large numbers of two-year-olds to choose from can usually find horses meeting the criteria. In addition, they were probably purchased for the kind of money necessary to win at Saratoga. A fairer indication of an animal's worth occurs in the fall and the subsequent spring.

Our experience fit the pattern. Winners started appearing in that fall and the spring of 2004. Saratoga County continued to train in his lackluster style, although he appeared to be trying a little harder in the afternoon. Now that he was running at the proper class level, the competition became stiffer. He started to fall back into his old habit of finding friends on the track. As you might suspect, the friendliest horses were usually in the back of the pack and he enjoyed joining them. George Weaver mentioned this tendency to Edgar Prado, who was riding Saratoga County in a race at Belmont. In the race, Saratoga stumbled out of the gate and was soundly bumped. Rather than get mad, he accepted the bump as a friendly one and wanted to chat about it. In any event, it wasn't until the half-way point that the eventual winner passed him. The competition woke him up and he began to run, finishing second, only one length off the winner.

Aside from his overly affable nature and his tendency to ignore jockeys' instructions, Saratoga was doing quite well. A near miss in his first race against allowance-level horses was considered a good performance and he was only a two-year-old. Early wins are important to the future value of a budding equine star. In a world intent on quick returns, a sire or a broodmare who can produce early winning babies is highly praised and well-compensated.

It was October and the Weaver barn was packing up for the trip to Florida. His string of trainees had shown some fairly good growth with a number of new owners coming on board. One of them shifted an entire barn of horses over to George's tutelage.

We had, at this point, moved the bulk of our horses to Weaver while retaining a few with other conditioners. It's the type of industry where baskets and eggs should always be considered, because events can cause attitudes to change quickly.

Saratoga County was happy to be back in Florida, especially in the pleasant Palm Meadows surroundings. His ball and his highway cone were in their proper positions and a tempting group of bitees were parading past his stall. The morning works were not too tasking and he had his usual cadre of old and new friends to run with on the track. Allison had returned with him to Florida, and that was a good thing. As usual she seemed to understand he was the boss, but a compassionate one.

George Weaver was plotting out a race program for Saratoga. After letting him recover from his near-claim experience up north, and allowing him to do some more growing, he was thinking graded stakes. Saratoga had grown quite a bit by the time the Spectacular Bid stakes was about to be run at Gulfstream Park. He was ready to go. His already powerful rear end had muscled up even more and he was beginning to look quite powerful. Unfortunately, he was as affable as ever.

John Velazquez was back on for the January 10th race. Saratoga County ambled over to the saddling paddock, managing to step on the edge of his foot and dislodge his shoe. This was a new trick he had just picked up. It always resulted in a flurry of activity, involving grooms and farriers and trainers. He just loved the hubbub. For everyone else, it was nerve-racking to be holding up the post parade of a major stakes race. Add to the mix the loud music from the bandstand near the saddling paddock and you had a lot of confusion. Saratoga County was the only one not confused. He calmly regarded the other horses. (None of them looked too tough.) Those nice owners were there along with Allison and the tall guy. What else could a horse ask for?

He could ask for a little more eye room. The tall guy had come over and slapped some blinkers on him; apparently designed to reduce his ability to see his other friends on the track. He was especially interested in watching this Win Dot Comma guy whom everyone was picking as the favorite. But his real target was Smokume, who had beaten him by a length at Belmont. He was doing a lot of bragging about that race as they were tacking up. (This was the kind of thing that could make a guy less affable.)

Saratoga County broke well this time and managed to be second by a head at the half-way point. (No lollygagging at the back when he had something to prove.) He hit the turn with Smokume on his inside. His nemesis started to move out on him, forcing Saratoga to float out as well, losing some precious steps. As a result, he finished second to the favorite by a length. He did, however, show up the other loudmouth.

102

After the race, George Weaver was quoted, "I thought he ran an excellent race, considering it was only his third start and he got floated off the last turn by Smokume. My colt likes to lay on horses a little bit, which is why I put blinkers on him. I could see he was thinking about the horse inside of him instead of where the wire was when he got carried out on the turn."

If Saratoga County could have read Weaver's remarks, his first reaction would have been, "So that's why I was wearing that dumb hood, and I didn't lay on him, he laid on me, and I always knew where the finish line was. I had to dispose of that dumb horse first."

What the race did prove was Saratoga could race at this level with the better horses. Distance was the next important consideration. The Spectacular Bid was six furlongs. The next natural step was the seven-furlong Hutcheson Stakes at Gulfstream on February 14th. The ultimate goal for good three-year-olds this time of year was, of course, the Kentucky Derby. In the case of Saratoga County, his looks and his pedigree did not make a convincing case, but in the racing business, anything can happen. It was Weaver's plan to test his horse at increasingly longer distances.

Saratoga was not thinking Kentucky Derby (he never heard of it anyway), but he must have thought, "This racing has been fun, and as long as they don't work me too hard in the morning, allow me adequate nap time, and keep me away from that Smokume guy, I'll be happy."

18

Florida

Fresh off his strong performance in the Spectacular Bid, Weaver started preparing Saratoga County for his next logical start, the Hutcheson Stakes at Gulfstream Park. In his last race, Saratoga County ran like he was starting to understand the game and even his morning workouts seemed to have more zip. The field looked strong, with Dogwood Stable's Limehouse from the powerful Todd Pletcher barn the likely favorite.

For his part, Saratoga couldn't see what all the fuss was about. Someone interviewed the tall guy after the last race and they appeared to be talking about him. Maybe he got a little too ticked-off, but he couldn't take it. That was an aggravating bunch. He vowed to be less aggressive in the next race, and try to get along with everybody.

We had lunch in the Turf Club before the race, basking in the glow of being one of the contenders. It seemed we had come a long way from having hamburgers with Norman and his girlfriend at Rockingham Park. The purse level was a bit higher and the trophy wasn't plastic. As we ate, we watched the owner of Deputy Storm let everybody within earshot know he was the owner of Deputy Storm. The horse was running in our race. We preferred to stay quiet until the race was run.

We waited in the saddling paddock, listening to this week's musical group holding forth. (They don't seem to make music the way they did when we were young.) Meanwhile, Saratoga County was doing his horseshoe act. He was followed by the usual group of grooms and farriers, intent on keeping his equipment in place. He looked as laid back as ever.

Coming out of the fourth post, he banged the gate and was checked early. As a result, he spotted the field ten lengths running down the backstretch. Eibar Coa never had ridden him and wasn't really tuned in to his style. Saratoga County was annoyed about all the ruckus around the starting gate, but he vowed to keep his promise about not losing his cool. He picked up a buddy and was content to run with him for the first half-mile. He didn't gain an inch on the leaders who were still well ahead. A frustrated Coa urged him to make a move without much luck. Saratoga decided to get in the game as they went into the turn, but by then it was far too late, and he finished up third, four lengths behind Limehouse after making a nice little closing move from the point where he decided to start running. No reporters were talking to the tall guy after this race, and Saratoga decided it was good he stayed so well-behaved.

We were all generally pleased with the race. Third place got us a $20,000 piece of the purse. (That would translate into five wins out of Norman at Rockingham and a lot of ice.) On the minus side, the Deputy Storm guy beat us with a second-place finish. We would have a chance to even the score later on.

The two Florida races convinced George Weaver his horse was a player and could run with the best of them. He was now faced with the decision about where to run Saratoga County next. His first thought was the Swale Stakes at Gulfstream. As it turned out, the Swale had only six entrants and we had Jerry Bailey to ride. George indicated he had entered to take a look at the field (an expensive look after paying the necessary fees), and then decided to go for the Gotham Stakes at Aqueduct. We had the feeling he had made his mind up before he entered, but went along with his decision. (How small a field and how good a jockey would he have needed to go with the Swale?)

When you get right down to it, owners aren't really in the business for the money. If they were, very few of them would be happy. The real drawing card, the one that attracts participants from every walk of life, was notoriety. Let's face it. What other major sport will allow older, out-of-shape folks to achieve the same recognition as other sports figures? The only drawback is the public pays little attention to all but a few major races every year. The most popular being the Kentucky Derby, the subsequent Triple Crown races, the Breeder's Cup races and, maybe, the Dubai World Cup races. Anytime you tell a non-race fan about your involvement in the racing business, the question is always the same, "Have you run in the Kentucky Derby yet?"

We got a small exposure to notoriety when George was interviewed after our second-place finish in the Spectacular Bid. The implied question in the interview, of course, was, "Do you plan to run in the Kentucky Derby?" Getting even that close was a real thrill for us.

Going for the Gotham was our attempt to answer those questions, if not for the press, at least for the owners. When George Weaver accompanied his horse on the plane to New York, he had plenty of time to consider his decision to skip the Swale, with its small field and Jerry Bailey. He also had time to admire Eddington, the big favorite in the Gotham, who shared the plane. "Eddington is a big, good-looking, impressive horse," he told the press. "Who knows? He may go on to win the Kentucky Derby. But I thought if he was going to be vulnerable, this, a one-turn, one mile race would be the spot."

George had lined up Javier Castellano to ride. He was an excellent jockey, just coming into his own with some major stakes races under his belt. He was also a patient rider who didn't try to force a horse into a running style he felt uncomfortable with. From our experience with Saratoga County, he seemed to have just the attitude we were looking for. Castellano commented on the Gotham. "He (George) showed me his last race (the Hutcheson) where he lugged out and hit the gate pretty hard. I told George, If he breaks clean, he wins the race."

From the pre-race hoopla, it became apparent we were about to enter a new tier of owners, provided, of course, we won the Gotham. (Maybe us fleas had found ourselves a big dog.)

19

New York

The Gotham was run on the first day of spring. It was a day that began as a fitting ending for winter, and a day that marked the beginning of the Kentucky Derby quest for a group of promising three-year-olds. In addition to the well-regarded Eddington, the race included Redskin Warrior, who had run a big one in his last start; the highly regarded Pomeroy; Deputy Storm, the runner-up in the Hutcheson, and Quick Action, trained by the legendary Wayne Lukas.

As the day progressed, winter began to return with darkening skies and a strong wind blowing in off Jamaica Bay. As Saratoga County sauntered around the paddock, his shoes still intact, he took the measure of his opponents. Eddington and Redskin Warrior were certainly big dudes and he remembered Deputy Storm from the Hutcheson. He figured he was going to avoid watching the rear-end of the latter horse in front of him, as he had in their last race.

As Saratoga was warming up on the track, without the customary company of a lead pony, George was commenting to the press.

"He's so lazy and easygoing, even at this stage of the game, I still have to gallop him in company, because he gets nothing out of his workout if he does it alone. It's a perfect-world situation when you have a racehorse who knows when to turn it on and doesn't beat himself in the morning." Saratoga County loaded into the gate without knowing he was in a perfect-world situation.

What surprised Saratoga was the way the wind carried him through the early stages of the race. Eddington got knocked sideways early, and his nemesis, Deputy Storm, was flying, chased by Pomeroy who was making his first start after a long layoff. The howling wind and the obvious seriousness of the horses around him banished any thoughts of chit-chatting from his mind. Above the din, he could hear the race caller on the loudspeaker getting more excited as the race progressed. Saratoga felt it was odd, because he wasn't running any harder than he usually ran.

Up ahead, Pomeroy was disposing of Deputy Storm and Eddington, and Redskin Warrior was still at the back of the pack. Saratoga felt he was moving faster and the announcer guy was getting more excited, so he went with the flow. Then he turned into the wind, and experienced something new: real resistance. It caused him to dig in and call on all the power he had in his muscular rump. He shot by Pomeroy, who didn't like the wind at all, and finished two lengths ahead. He had no idea what happened to the other horses who had looked so good in the paddock.

George Weaver, soft-spoken in his daily interactions, has a tendency to let it go when he sees one of his charges do well on the track. In this case, he bolted for the winner's circle (not quite as fast as he did when Saratoga won his first start).

The horse saw him coming, followed by the press, and knew he had done a good thing today.

"I'm at a loss for words," the tall guy was saying. "I can hardly talk. I can't believe it. It's like a dream to me." Saratoga County now knew what a perfect-world situation really was.

In the winner's circle, George was generous with his praise. "I'm so grateful to all the people that work for me, especially my wife, Cindy. She's the one who does all the work and rides all the projects and the wackos." (All those projects and wackos are probably the other horses George bought for us over the years.)

In our quest for notoriety, and Weaver's quest for new clients, the Gotham was a big step forward. Steve Haskin, writing in *The Blood-Horse,* had the best description of the race. "Racing's *Good Book of Trainers* might read something like this-'And so Lukas begat Pletcher and Pletcher begat Weaver and Weaver went out unto the land of Queens and vanquished both Lukas and Pletcher, as well as two of the purported saviors of the 2004 Kentucky picture.' "

The headlines told the rest of the story:

The Thoroughbred Times—"Saratoga County stakes his claim. Valid Expectations colt defeats Pomeroy and Eddington in Gotham and could be headed for Kentucky."

Daily Racing Form—"Weaver makes right move."

Associated Press—"County win may point him toward Derby."

Blood Horse—"Saratoga County mows 'em down late."

South Florida Sun Sentinel—"Saratoga County surprises in Gotham."

The Saratogian—"Saratoga County a winner."

(Note the interest reflected in the last two, our hometown papers. The notoriety thing was beginning to kick in.)

Derby fever now began to shift into high gear. The interviews all began moving in that direction. Richard Rosenblatt of the *Associated Press* asked this question "Saratoga County can win at Aqueduct. Is Churchill Downs in his future? The three-year-old colt swept to the lead turning for home and won the $200,000 Gotham Stakes yesterday, giving trainer George Weaver a glimmer of hope for a starter in the Kentucky Derby on May 1. Before the mile-long Gotham, Weaver said Saratoga County was not a Derby horse, but the win over Derby prospects Eddington and Redskin Warrior may have the trainer reassessing his plans."

" 'This was a terrific win for him,' Weaver said, 'let me see how he handles two turns. I'm not sure he's a Kentucky Derby horse. Most of the big races are April 10 at 1 1/8 miles, but they come up too soon.' George opted for the Lexington Stakes at Kentucky on April 17. The race was 1 1/16 miles with a $325,000 purse. 'The Lexington is the right step,' Weaver said. 'Horses have run in the Lexington and gone on to the Kentucky Derby.' "

20

Kentucky

George Weaver's barn usually moves to Kentucky for a while each year in deference to his ties to the region and his parents being located there. In 2004, he had another reason to make the stop. Saratoga County was to run in the Coolmore Lexington. Fourteen horses were entered with eight of them considered Derby candidates. Four others were looking to make enough money to qualify. Our horse was right in between. He was twentieth on the graded stakes earnings list, with $156,500 in the bank. A good performance in the Lexington would get him in.

The most important question remaining was whether Saratoga could make the 1 1/4 mile Derby distance. Weaver was anxious to see how he would handle his first route race. During a nationally broadcast teleconference Weaver said, "We figured this would be the kind of race that would tell us if we needed to do something like that. I don't want to make the mistake of writing the horse off before we even know for sure. There's a lot of horses that their pedigrees and other things like running styles indicate they don't want to go that far, but they end up doing it anyway. We'll evaluate the race in Lexington and he'll let us know what he wants to do and when he's ready to do it." Knowing Saratoga County's outlook on life, I suspect his answer to a direct question of this type would have been, "Sure, what the hell, I'll try anything once."

We loaded up the car for an early return to the North with a stopover in Kentucky. The side trip also gave us the opportunity to visit a farm in the area that was home to Fortunate Card, a stakes-winning mare of ours who had just given birth to a colt. The mare had won the Desert Vixen Stakes at Calder and was retired with a bone chip.

While we were on the road, we kept in touch with the post position drawing for the Lexington. We knew we were going into the race with a pedigree strike against us and hoped a good post might improve our chances. The track at Keenland was fairly narrow, with a short run to the first turn.

The draw turned out badly. We were fourteen in a field of fourteen with little chance of establishing a decent position in the early going. We had gone this far, however, and there was no turning back.

Race day was cool and sunny and the track was fast. We were struck with the carefree attitude of the spectators. Kentuckians really love their racing. We were also amazed by the lack of restrictions around the barn area. Coming from the Northeast, we were used to being hassled by security when we tried to get near the animals you shelled out a bunch of money to acquire. Keeping track of all the pictures and badges required was a full-time job. At breakfast, the morning of the race, we mentioned to some people at our hotel we had a horse in the big race. When we got to the backside, there was Saratoga County trying his best to bite the same people we had been talking to.

The saddling procedure, with throngs of people in the paddock, was quite chaotic. Everyone seemed to be having a good time and Saratoga had plenty of people to watch. He fought his way through the crowd and headed for the track. Now a veteran of many races and many tracks, he calmly surveyed the starting gate. One look at his position in the gate led him to suspect something was wrong. He seemed to be right on the rail, but the rail was on his wrong side and a large tractor appeared to be parked right in front of him. He took it all as a new experience.

Because of the short run to the first turn, the field hit it in a pack. Saratoga was still near the outside rail on the turn and he settled into the tenth position going down the backstretch only six lengths off the lead. He passed horses, but couldn't shake his outside path. He reached the final turn only three lengths off the lead, but five wide with no chance to make up any ground in the stretch. He finished seventh beaten fourteen lengths. Actually, not a bad performance, given the conditions he had to deal with. It convinced George (not that he really needed to be convinced) the Derby was not in Saratoga's future, and he had to settle for life as a sprinter.

As you might suspect, with Saratoga County off the Kentucky Derby trail, the press dropped him like a hot potato. We all went back to the business of owning and running horses at the upcoming Saratoga Springs meet.

Saratoga's interest in racing seemed to diminish at this point. He understood, somewhere down deep, he had missed the big dance. No one was interviewing the tall guy anymore and new pictures of him in action stopped appearing in the office at the barn. "In a way, it might be a good thing," he said to himself. "Now I can settle down to a more comfortable routine, easy works in the morning, and new friends to run with in the afternoon."

His record through the summer seemed to reflect that attitude. Saratoga didn't run badly—a fourth in the Withers Stakes—a fifth in the Kings Bishop Stakes—a fourth in the Jerome Stakes. He was bringing in a check each time he ran, but not coming very close to winning. His forte continued to be closing, because he was still spending the early part of the race socializing. Try as he might, Weaver couldn't break him of the habit. He finally gave up and counted on maturity doing the trick.

Javier Castellano was a frequent rider, but others also pitched in. The most interesting race during this period was the one with Jerry Bailey up. Jerry was one of the best jockeys to ever ride and he did it, in part, by being in command of the race. One thing previous riders had told us about Saratoga County was he didn't like to be commanded. In fact, he hardly paid any attention to the jockey at all. (One of the reasons for many of his weaker performances.) When the gate opened, it was clear that backstretch socializing was out, and Saratoga County was in for a tough day. He responded with an eleven-lengths loss. I can imagine the horse said to himself after the race, "Who was that guy?"

Toward the fall of the year, Saratoga County started to show a little more life. He finished second in allowance races at Belmont and Keeneland, but he was still running below his potential. Weaver began to think lay-off, a vacation at some farm until the spring. Saratoga was about to turn four and suffer one of the biggest class jumps a horse can take, from three-year-old to four-year-old and up races. The upgrade is equivalent to a high school athlete moving to the college level. Simply put, now Saratoga County would have a lot more competition at the top level. There was an allowance race for him scheduled at Churchill Downs before the end of the year, so we took a shot and entered him. Easily the most important decision George Weaver made during Saratoga County's brief career.

21

Other Runners

No matter how well one of your horses is doing (and Saratoga County was really doing well), your other runners continue to deserve a good deal of your attention. We own a nifty filly named Pelham Bay, a New York-bred Pat Kelly picked out for us in the 2003 Saratoga Springs yearling sale. We went down to Belmont to watch her win first time out in a two-year-old race. Still glowing from the win, we headed back North. Before we got through the Pelham Bay section of New York, for which she was named, Kelly called us with an offer to buy her.

The issue of when to sell a horse, or to sell one at all, is always present. The philosophy of many horse breeders and pinhookers is to have the horse up for sale at all times—as a weanling, as a yearling, as a two-year-old, as a race horse off the track. It gives them multiple opportunities to unload at a profit, especially when the animal is maturing slowly. Many buyers feel purchasing a horse that has shown something on the track is the best way to acquire a future star. The overall horsemen's philosophy is: "Better to be sorry you sold, than sorry you didn't."

A good example is the yearling sales at the Saratoga summer meet, where well-heeled buyers gather to spend big bucks on select horses. Is it sensible for them to spend a million dollars on a horse that still has to be broken and trained before you can determine if it moves sufficiently well to be a winner? The alternative would be to walk over to the track and claim a horse that might help you reach your goal.

In addition, many trainers have the bad habit of giving up too early on their trainees, making them targets for shrewd claimers. Saratoga County was the poster boy for that approach. Seventy-five thousand dollars invested in our horse when he ran his initial maiden claimer would have brought a huge return to the new owner (and a really depressed George Weaver). Putting a promising horse in a claiming race is, of course, a calculated decision, as is weighing an offer to buy your horse outright. When a horse is claimed, it's a buyer beware situation, because it can't be returned if physical problems exist. One purchased directly can be carefully examined.

There are other factors to be considered when dealing with a purchase offer. If you are in the business to sell rather than race, it comes down to price. If you are in to race, it's a different matter. The best guideline I've heard for this situation is to ask yourself "knowing the animal as well as I do, would I buy it for the price I am being offered?" If the answer is no, then by all means, sell it. The resulting cash flow can be used to buy other promising horses. However, if Evelyn is in your equation, and she loves the horse, than you had better keep it, or be prepared for a lot of pain and suffering.

We held on to Pelham Bay and it turned out to be the right decision. She won a stakes for New York bred two-year-olds at Belmont in the fall and finished second in two non-restricted stakes in the winter. She tries hard and provides the racing entertainment we are looking for while covering her costs. (What else could we ask for?)

Another spunky little horse we had claimed away from us was named Missile Bay. We thought her name was a clever play on words, because it allowed us to stay within our traditional county and bay system and branch out a bit. We named her after the section of our nuclear submarines that houses its intercontinental missiles. We thought it was an appropriate name for this quick little filly who was called the pocket rocket by the people that trained her. She was fast, but without much staying power. Missile Bay was doing OK, however, running in short races. Weaver put her in a $75,000 claimer and she was claimed.

Missile, subsequently, went on to win several small stakes at the mid-Atlantic tracks, prompting George to admit, "I guess we left a little too much meat on the bones" (more trainer speak). As usual my financial background kicked in and I started evaluating whether the claim was a good or a bad thing. The secret is to follow the purse revenue of the claimed horse less the expenses you would have accumulated and see if the $75,000 claiming price holds up. To date we are still about $10,000 ahead of the game, but we lost the entertainment value.

We had many horses claimed over the years with Missile Bay the only one we really regretted. Others, such as Middlesex County, a head case, is an example. He looked good. A gray gelding who ran fairly well, but couldn't walk or gallop (an all or nothing animal). Months after we lost him, exercise riders came around to the barn, asking how we got him to walk and gallop. The answer was, we didn't. (That was why the new owner got a $100,000 horse for $15,000.)

Another horse, a personal favorite of Evelyn, was claimed (with all the attendant pain and suffering) from Pat Kelly. Her name was Paugus Bay, another cute little filly, who had a habit of getting lost in the pack because of her size and surprising the jockeys on the bigger horses who said they never saw her coming. She was so small, in fact, that windy days affected her performance. In one race, we thought she had been bumped on the turn, but found out later she was taken out by a gust of wind. As with Missile Bay, we counted on her size to discourage would-be claimers. Many times Kelly would notice people looking her over in the saddling paddock, but turning away when they saw how small she was. Little fillies also tend to discourage trainers looking for a potential broodmare.

The miracle of modern technology makes it possible for you to kick yourself over and over for good horses you lost or for successful horses you might have had if you made the right choice at the horse auction. It never seems to fail, the one you choose turns out to be a dud, while the one you rejected turns out to be a stakes winner. George Weaver can quote the exploits of those horses all day long, while we watch the runners we did buy bucking and dodging around the track.

Occasionally, you can pick up a relatively low-priced horse at an auction and get almost instant gratification. Henry Collazo selected Fortunate Card at a two-year old-sale in Ocala and instantly declared she would win in the Florida Stallion Stakes to be held in the summer. She was a daughter of Fortunate Prospect, a popular local stallion. We, of course, took his promise with the same grain of salt we did with all trainer predictions. Hall of Fame jockey Pat Day rode Card in her initial race, so we thought we might have something. Unable to see the race (Evelyn had forced open my tight purse strings for a cruise to Alaska), we got the results after the race on the ship's internet. Noting a second place finish, not bad for her first try, we assumed Day had worked his magic. Collazo was not so sure Day was all that much help. We got a a purchase offer right after the race well in-excess of the $20,000 we paid for the horse, but remembering Henry's promise, decided to wait for the lucrative Stallion Stakes series.

We watched Fortunate Card win the first leg of the series by a head in a stirring stretch duel. Evelyn was standing in the Saratoga racing office when her horse won. A reporter from the Florida Horse was in the office as well. Henry Collazo ended up with the most glowing owner's comments ever recorded in print.

Fortunate Card finished third in the next leg of the series and out of the money in the third after leading most of the way. She retired shortly thereafter with a bone chip in her knee (possibly the reason we got her so cheaply at the sale). Card was well worth the entertainment value and she even made a few bucks.

We decided to keep her as a broodmare because she was a stakes winner with a good pedigree. Everything that goes around comes around. We were now back in the breeding business Something we had vowed never to do again, but it gave us an outlet for placing horses at the end of their racing career.

22

Horse Disposal

Fortunate Card was the first horse we retained as a brood-mare (and I swore she would be the last). Although Card was quite young, she turned out to be a good mother. She raised her first baby, a colt by More Than Ready, on a pleasant farm in Kentucky. Her second breeding, to the same sire, produced a tough little filly. It was a hard delivery that resulted in complications (just what we hated down on the farm when we were in the broodmare business).

The strategy of breeding back to the same sire each year is an interesting one. Most mare owners look for diversity and are constantly in the search for hot stallions at a cheap price. We felt if you planned to run the first foal yourself, you had the ability to influence the value of the second and third foals. Full brothers and sisters of successful runners are very well received at the sales. What's required, of course, is the success of the first foal (many times an elusive goal). Like everything else in the horse business, you pay your money and you take your chances.

Fortunate Card never did recover from her last hard birthing and had to be euthanized. Apparently, she suffered nerve damage from the difficult extraction and lost her ability to stand.

Like every other promise I made to myself, the further avoidance of the breeding business proved short-lived. We had purchased a big, beautiful, gray filly by Two Punch and named her Camden Bay. She had a good pedigree and good conformation. The one thing she lacked was soundness. Camden suffered from a series of injuries that prevented her from breaking her maiden in a timely manner.

One day a painter, a friend of one of Pat Kelly's assistants, showed up to do a barn scene. Pat's Saratoga stalls were located in a pretty spot next to the Yaddo Gardens. It was an ideal place for painting. Unfortunately, the horse she chose to paint against this background was Camden Bay, in all her physical glory. The result was a masterpiece. (She really was a good artist.) A few weeks later, the painter showed up on our doorstep, with a big, impressive oil in a fancy gold frame. As you might expect, Evelyn snatched it right up for the bargain price of $3,000.

About the same time, one of Camden's nagging injuries worsened to the point where racing was no longer a viable option. Now that the painting was hanging proudly in our dining room, making Camden Bay officially one of Evelyn's favorite horses, my alternative of giving her away disappeared (the horse, not Evelyn). Camden now resides at the McMahon farm in Saratoga Springs, where she has already given birth to a precocious little filly by Judge TC. She is in foal again to the same stallion. (Once I get a strategy, I never change it.)

This leads directly to the problem of dealing with horses that can no longer race, but are healthy enough to lead a long life. Over the years, we have had to face this issue many times (forty-five to be exact). Getting your horse claimed is one approach, but it just pushes the problem on to a new owner. Many times you can find someone who is anxious to accept your animal as a riding horse, but the temperament of a Thoroughbred is not always ideal for the new occupation. Trainers are usually happy to replace an unproductive horse in their barn with a better runner and will be happy to help out. We have, over the years, accepted assurances our horses are running across pristine fields in retirement, but it may have just been wishful thinking. Overriding all of this is the specter of the slaughter of race horses.

Every owner should be concerned with the eventual fate of the animals they buy. When you consider the number of foals registered each year, their ultimate disposition becomes a real issue. Until the U.S. Tax Reform Act of 1986 was passed, the number had been increasingly rapidly. The combined total of Thoroughbred, Quarter Horse, and Arabian registered foals in 1975 was 141,108. By 1985, the total had risen by 75 percent to 237,797. The Reform Act eliminated the liberal investment tax credits and passive loss limitation rules that helped inflate the foal totals. The liberal tax treatments allowed millions of dollars to be pumped into horse owning syndicates, breeding and racing operations.

With the change, the number of foals registered on an annual basis began to drop immediately. However, the damage was done. With large numbers of animals now requiring maintenance that had become financially burdensome, owners began looking for a way out of the business. They could sell their horses or give them away (but with too many sellers and not enough buyers, this was not a great option). They could have their horses put down (euthanized) or they could sell the horses for slaughter.

To separate the last two options, it's important to discuss the role money plays in the equation. Euthanasia is a form of disposal that costs the owner out-of-pocket. It's estimated the expense of lethal injection can range from $50 to $150, to which you add another $100 to $200 to move the carcass for disposal. The carcass can be cremated, which has its own additional cost along with the problem of locating a facility large enough, or the carcass can be shipped to a rendering plant. There are 285 such plants located across the country, but transportation costs and fees are also involved. The slaughter option is the only one where, rather than costing the owner, there is some income available.

Rendering is the use of various animal parts for a variety of nonhuman consumption purposes. The standard attitude is exemplified by a sitcom episode I remember where one of the characters was attempting to distribute her uncle's ashes in the winner's circle at Belmont Park. Her husband found a friend who was racing a horse there and got him to agree to the distribution, if he won. When assessing his friend's chance of winning, he asked the horse's name and was told—Soon to be Glue (not a great sign). The fact is, horse derived glue is no longer popular. Brands like Elmer's are predominate because they can use derivatives from the dairy cow business (this ranks them right up there on the Buddy Leroux scale of vertical integration). Dog food products have gone in the same direction, after they were forced to display the contents on the cans. Apparently, the consuming public balked at the idea of feeding my friend Flicka to Fido.

This leaves human consumption, primarily overseas, in Europe and Japan, as the main users of horsemeat. Because lethal injection is not an option, other non-humane methods are utilized. Add to that the financial realities of the horsemeat business and you have a very unpalatable solution to the horse disposal problem.

The financial side is clear. A horse purchased for $500 receives, on average, $600 from the plant, leaving a $100 margin that must cover the cost of transportation. To make the deal work, horses are crammed into double-deck vans. You can imagine how hard this is on the animals.

One main source of horses is the auctions. We were always aware of "the killers," and made sure we set our reserve price above their highest economic purchase level. Many sellers do not have the same motivation.

Thanks to the awareness of this situation, the number of horses slaughtered for human consumption each year has declined steadily. The number in the United States has dropped from 348,400 in 1987 to 40,000 in 2002. Some breeders are now offering to buy back their horses at a price above the kill level if it is the owner's only option. We got such an offer with the foal papers of our stakes winning New York-bred, Pelham Bay, when we bought her as a yearling. Organizations have sprung up to take horses that would normally go through the slaughter process. One of them, the Thoroughbred Retirement Foundation, goes as far as visiting killer pens at the auctions and buying back horses at a price that covers the profit margin.

Horses rescued from the auctions or acquired elsewhere are either placed on the foundation's farms or adopted out to people who have been thoroughly screened. The Thoroughbred Retirement Foundation's prison programs have turned out to be an ideal outlet, because it gives the inmates something to focus on that can become a future vocation. (Not a bad idea given the caliber of people we were forced to deal with during our breeding farm years.) Horses rescued in this manner sometimes turn out to have some degree of fame. It was the alleged slaughter of 1986 Kentucky Derby winner Ferdinand in Japan that sparked a good deal of reaction against the slaughter business. It's hard to determine the true numbers involved, but it could be argued that since 1989 as many as 2,500,000 horses that might otherwise have perished in the slaughterhouses have not done so.

We had the opportunity to get involved with the Foundation on a personal basis. George Weaver selected a two-year-old for us, a colt named Palm Beach County (a name chosen by our granddaughter who wanted to call him Palmy). The horse was training well and looked to have a fairly good future when he took a bad step and broke a bone. The first reaction from the hard-hearted banker was to put him down, but warm racing hearts prevailed and he was operated on in Kentucky. The argument that the break was clean and he might recover was diluted when the screw broke and he had to be re-operated on and have his bone wrapped with wire. Four months later the horse was still badly lame without much chance of being given away as a riding horse, not to mention ever running again. The Thoroughbred Retirement Foundation was the answer. We contribute $2,500 annually and we got the opportunity to send them the horse. Palmy will lead a useful life and our granddaughter is happy.

We believe it is the owner's responsibility to consider the ultimate disposition of the animals that provide so much in the way of joy and entertainment, no matter how profitable or unprofitable the business has been.

23

The Comeback

It's hard to tell what happened to Saratoga County. George Weaver would subsequently indicate it was a change in his training schedule. Maturity may have kicked in, or it could just be the horse overheard a lot of talk about a hiatus (whatever that is), and a stay at a horse farm somewhere. Saratoga was not going to be separated from Allison, the tall guy, or even the cute little woman who seems to have a stake in him. Maybe he thought it was time to get serious about racing.

In any event, he went into the November 27, seven-furlong allowance race at Churchill Downs with a whole new outlook on life. It was closing day at the venerable old track. He recalled a big issue about his running there earlier in the year, but nothing ever came of it. He had Joe Johnson on his back, a kid he had never met. He seemed friendly enough, but it didn't matter, because his plan was to take solid control of his career and make sure he wasn't going to some farm away from his folks. A glance at the tote board (he was five to one) told him the bettors were disrespecting him. Didn't they realize what a weak bunch of runners he was up against? The favorite, St. Averil, hadn't run in nearly eight months and the rest were beatable.

Saratoga County got away from the gate cleanly and was running four wide down the backstretch. This time he had no interest in fooling around with other horses. He moved quickly to the front, passing the dueling leaders and blowing the field away by five-and-a-half lengths. We were watching at home on TVG where the commentator described his race as "freakishly fast."

After the race, Joe Johnson commented he thought Saratoga had made his move too early. He tried to convey his feelings to the horse, who ignored him completely. Saratoga County had become a horse on a mission.

Any thoughts of a layoff had left Weaver's mind to be replaced with visions of grandeur. Always a trainer not afraid to ship, George prepared him to run in the Malibu Stakes in California. The horse had flown before, up from Florida for the Gotham, but he had never done it on Federal Express. (Come to think of it, neither have I.) Well, there it was, a huge cargo plane with a giant lift and a pallet ready to carry Saratoga skyward and into the cargo hold. Saratoga took one look at all the equipment and said, "No thanks." Shortly thereafter, George Weaver watched the van pull up returning his horse to the barn and shrugged it off as another Saratoga County decision.

It turned out to be the right decision. The plane, along with another horse bound for the same race, got as far as Texas, where it got snowed in and remained. Both horses were scratched. It appeared that along with a new outlook on life Saratoga had acquired a sixth sense (one that also helped him figure out where the finish line was and how to get there in time).

With his traveling days over, at least for now, Saratoga began training for his next race, the Mr. Prospector Stakes at Gulfstream Park. It was to be a much tougher race, against top-tier sprinters, Limehouse, who beat him in the Hutchinson, and Wando, the Canadian champion.

Handicapper Mike Watchmaker, writing in the *Racing Form*, had a favorable view of Saratoga's chances. "There is

128

plenty of serious speed in this race," he wrote. "Half of the ten horses entered do their best running when on or right near the lead. That being the case, I want a horse who can capitalize if the race falls apart late, and the horse to do that is Saratoga County. He comes into this off by far the best performance of his career, a romp in an allowance race at Churchill Downs. The victory came at the expense of a much softer field than Saratoga County faces on Saturday, but the 108 Beyers figure he earned is the best last-out Beyer in this field. And, two bullet workouts since arriving in Florida say Saratoga County maintains that sharp form."

In unveiling this new version of his horse, George Weaver described his amended training technique. "He's always been a talented horse," he said, "but he's also been a horse who is lazy in the mornings. Sometimes, he'll give you 100 percent, but other times riders will tell him they have no horse when another comes to him, then he'll kick in again. So, I started giving him sharp works in the morning."

Javier Castellano, who rode some of those sharp early works, added, "I worked this horse at fifty-seven seconds (for five furlongs). I have never worked a horse that fast, so I was a little worried that maybe he worked too fast. But he's just that type of horse. He likes you to get into him and work him."

Gulfstream Park was going through a complete renovation in the winter of 2005 and none of the original structures were standing. The real plus was the disappearance of the bandstand and all those fine musicians it usually featured (the horses didn't miss them at all). For the Mr. Prospector, there was a good gathering of the industry elites. J.J. Pletcher, Todd's father, who we knew quite well from our farm days in Ocala, was there to welcome Limehouse back from his layoff. Several big-time New York trainers were there as well. We all watched on a billboard-sized television next to the saddling paddock. After the gates opened, we lost all sight of our horse as the pack ran down the backstretch.

On the track Saratoga County was boxed in nine lengths from the lead in tenth. He continued to the half-way mark in the same position and Castellano started to worry about the effect of the overly fast workout. Suddenly Saratoga picked his head up. He moved to the outside, used his newly acquired sixth sense to smell out the finish line, and took off. He rounded the turn five wide without losing momentum and (to use an old expression) passed the field like they were standing still. He won by two-and-a-half lengths and set a new track record of 1:08.99. After the race Castellano was heard saying, "I wondered when he was going to start running." (Good old Saratoga, always in command.)

Watching on the big screen, we all wondered if our horse was going to show up at all. When his white-bridled head appeared, we perked up and when he roared past the field, pandemonium broke loose. After the race Evelyn said, "I love this horse like a person. This race was unbelievable. He's never that far back. He's got a mind of his own and a big, big engine. He loves to run, but it's usually on his own schedule." George Weaver commented, "I think this performance should put to rest any thoughts people might have had that his Gotham win was a fluke."

In the winner's circle the trophy was presented by Tony Sirico, better known as Pauly Walnuts of "The Sopranos" popular television series. When Evelyn said she never heard of him or his show (we have separate television sets), Sirico grabbed her by both cheeks and exclaimed, "George, is this the kind of face that would watch 'The Sopranos?' " (I think not.) To show the small world horsemen live in, Sirico and several other cast members share an interest in a horse called Caramooch from the same mare as our New York-bred Boundary Bay.

Weaver now turned his attention to scheduling the next race. We were clearly on a roll and it looked like the elusive fame and fortune goal was getting closer and closer. Two more stakes races were available in a series for sprinters at Gulfstream, but there was also the General George at Laurel Park. The Maryland race would feature Don Six, runaway winner of two stakes races at Aqueduct. He was being touted as the fastest sprinter in the country. If asked, I'm sure Saratoga County would have said, "Bring the sucker on."

24

Maryland

Saratoga County had two consecutive impressive victories under his belt, and he beat some pretty good horses along the way. The Gulfstream people were interested in keeping him there for the Deputy Minister, but Weaver's mind was elsewhere. The General George offered twice the purse money, but more importantly, the opportunity to take on the self-professed best six-furlong horse in the country.

Don Six's trainer, Scott Lake, said before the race the only way his horse could not win was an act of God or if the race was cancelled because of snow.

Saratoga County may have heard about this fast Maryland horse through the grapevine (assuming horses have a grapevine), and he was ready. He caught and passed some good runners in the Mr. Prospector and he believed in his new strategy—look them in the eye in the stretch and they back down. (That's when he's not cozying up to them.)

George Weaver was on a newly found religious kick that got stronger every time he looked at his big horse. "I tell everybody around the barn I love him like a son," Weaver would say. "When I go to his stall, I'm so proud of him it's unbelievable. The feeling after he won the Gotham—I was beside myself. Even though he went a while between wins after that, every time I look at him , it gives me a good feeling inside. He's a nice, nice horse. Somebody told me Scott Lake said it would take an act of God for his horse to get beat, that's why I'm looking up."

Evelyn and I were looking up as well. It had been a long time since the Gotham. As pragmatic owners, it's dry periods like this when you watch the relentless buildup of training, vet, and van bills, with little or no offset from purse distributions and you realize it's a rich man's game. George never lost faith in his horse, no matter how much it cost us.

When the gate opened, Don Six did his thing, he went right to the lead and opened up a five-length advantage. The local announcer, working himself into a frenzy, proclaimed, "The blazing speed of Don Six." Mike Luzzi, the horse's jockey, fought gamely to hold Don Six in check as he sensed the open track in front of him and turned it on. He zipped through a quarter mile in 22.33 and a half in 44.97. Meanwhile, Saratoga County was running four-wide with the rest of the field, which included local favorite Gators and Bears. Saratoga County had his wild eye fixed on the leader and split the pack on the turn, beginning a grinding, relentless run to make up ground.

"As we approached the quarter pole, I was very confident," recalled Weaver. "It looked like Don Six was running out of steam, and I was like—this is great, he's a six-furlong horse, this is over. Then all of a sudden he kept running. I was pretty concerned when he dug in and I didn't think we were going to get there."

Javier Castellano was whipping him left-handed to keep him from lugging over on Don Six (a habit of his in the stretch). The effect of Saratoga County moving to the center of the track was part of the apparent surge of Don Six late in the race. The track announcer was back in a frenzy, "Oh, the courage of Don Six."

Meanwhile, back in the jockeys' room at Belmont Park, the assembled crowd of jockeys was on their feet, shouting in unison, "Right stick, Javier, right stick." At that point Castellano took the whip in his right hand and and straightened Saratoga out as the finish line flashed by. He won by a nose.

As he was galloping out, I'm sure Saratoga County was breathing a big sigh of relief. That sucker wasn't as easy to beat as he thought, but with the tall guy looking to the heavens and the cute little owner hiding in the bathroom down in Florida, how could he lose?

Our horse had brought us a long way in a relatively short time. We were now presented with some different issues. With the General George behind us the question of sire duty was before us. Several Kentucky farms began nosing around with some preliminary offers in the $750,000 range. Putting your horse out to stud is one of the ultimate goals of the business. When buyers pay multimillion dollar amounts for yearlings, they are clearly looking beyond purse money for the ultimate return on investment. A wildly successful sire like Storm Cat gets $500,000 for every foal he fathers. That kind of return certainly justifies a high price tag for a young prospect. The problem is, the lottery has much better odds than does the average owner to reap these rewards. Not only does a horse have to demonstrate outstanding ability on the track, but he has to do it while displaying an impeccable pedigree. Saratoga County was demonstrating some real ability, but his earning power was compromised by a rather average background. He was one of those horses who had to develop his own pedigree from scratch. Saratoga County was prepared to do just that. In addition, he had been showing some interest in the distaff side of the barn, as if anticipating what all his heroics on the racetrack might lead to.

George Weaver had several choices of what to do next. The Carter Handicap was the most obvious way to go. Saratoga needed a big win to fill out his resume and the New

York surroundings were close and comfortable for him. The ultimate test for a sprinter would be the Breeder's Cup in the fall with its $1 million purse and its cloak of prestige. On the way, there were stakes races at Saratoga Springs and Belmont Park before the big race.

The choice George made knocked us off our proverbial pins. He was opting for the Dubai World Cup races in the United Arab Emirates. This for a horse that already declined a flight to California. When asked by the press, George explained, "It's pretty much for the money. You're sending your horse and personnel around the world, so it's a pain in the butt. But they do put up the expenses and there just aren't enough opportunities for that kind of money between now and the Breeder's Cup. That's tough to ignore."

What was also tough to ignore was the way George Weaver was adjusting to the economics of the horse business. As an assistant to Lukas and Pletcher, he didn't have to deal with the financial pressures a trainer, on his own, faces. We take some pride in our contribution to his education, with our use of the report card with its emphasis on total cost numbers as well as its full disclosure of the financial performance of every horse bought at the auctions. Of course, having to meet a payroll and a feed bill each month also contributed.

We agreed with his decision. George had been right about going to the Gotham and the General George. Maybe good things do come in threes. I was about to replace a hip. (My second one. A logical consequence of a youth playing basketball and a middle aged man running marathons.) It seemed like a good excuse to avoid a long plane trip (not my favorite thing), and anyway, we can see the race much more clearly on our television set . After we had assembled enough flimsy excuses, we decided to stay home. When the press suggested we would be sorry if our horse won and we weren't there, I replied, "If we lose, it's a long, lonely trip home, and if we win, we wouldn't care where we were."

Another plus for running in Dubai was the presence of Pico Central. He was a champion sprinter whose loss in the 2004 Breeder's Cup cost him the Eclipse Award. His owners and many in the press felt he deserved that award, so he had something to prove. After a long layoff they had chosen the Golden Shaheen in Dubai (our race) as his platform.

The situation was not new to us after facing Limehouse in the same position and Don Six in the last race. In both cases, we were relatively unnoticed as the second or third choice in the betting. To make our also-ran position more certain, the owners of Pico Central ran a series of full-page, full-color advertisements in the *Thoroughbred Times*, extolling the past successes and future prospects of their horse. They concluded with the declaration, "On to Dubai."

Again, if Saratoga County could read, he would have commented, "Won't these guys ever wise up. I won't let them beat me no matter how much they pitch their horses."

As usual, Saratoga County wasn't consulted about the trip. He was busy eyeing fillies and working up an interest in the sire business. He did notice an increased interest in him in recent months, with a bunch of Kentucky-looking guys poking at him and dodging his attempts to grab their clothing. In fact, it was their ability to avoid his grabs that made him think they were Kentucky guys. Anyway, his biggest adventure was about to begin, whether he was ready or not.

25

Across the Globe

On Saturday March 26, 2005, Sheikh Mohammed Rashid al Maktoum, the crown prince of Dubai, welcomed the international racing community to Nad al Sheba Racecourse for the tenth running of the Dubai World Cup races. Dubai is located in the United Arab Emirates on the Persian Gulf near Saudi Arabia in a strategic part of the Middle East. Over the years, wealthy horse owners from this region have spread their influence around the world, as evidenced by their purchases of top-class yearlings in our sales, much like the $9.7-million colt mentioned earlier. As their influence grew so did the quality of horses traveling to Nad al Sheba each year. Runners such as Cigar, Silver Charm, Captain Steve, Street Cry, and Pleasantly Perfect have won major races there, even though they were forced to face a grueling travel experience to attend.

Races that began as a diversion for local horse owners had blossomed into a truly world class event that has come to equal (and some say surpass) the North American racing found in the Triple Crown and the Breeder's Cup races. Steve Crist, writing in the *Daily Racing Form*, opined on the growing quality of the Dubai World Cup event and the fact its importance is often overlooked while we concentrate on our domestic racing scene.

The significance of Dubai and the Golden Shaheen, publicized as the richest sprint race in the world, was not lost on the Weaver racing team as it prepared to begin another grand venture. Saratoga County got the feeling something big was afoot. The tall guy was particularly solicitous. More people were popping their wary heads into his stall and Allison looked like a woman preparing for a long trip.

Allison Logan, at the age of twenty-seven, was already an accomplished rider, having worked for Todd Pletcher before she settled in with George and Cindy. George, always aware of good omens, had her exercising all our horses, mindful of the success he had to date with Saratoga County. She and Saratoga began packing up their gear for the trip to Dubai. For Allison, it meant her riding gear and her sleeping bag, for Saratoga County it meant his rubber ball and his orange highway cone. In addition, they took a two-week supply of his feed (any change in diet could affect a horse negatively).

The plane was large and quite spacious, but most importantly, it had a long ramp to the door, allowing Saratoga comfortable access. (No Federal Express lift mechanism.) He breathed a sigh of relief. He was even happier when he saw the lay of the land. There were only four horses on the big plane. His groom Louie was there as was his best friend Allison and one other female exerciser-type. Saratoga County was glad of that because he just loved company, especially women.

One of the four horses was the Dale Romans-trained Roses in May, the favorite in the featured race, along with Liz, his exercise rider. We all dodged a bullet early, because an infection had been spreading around the barns and Romans' horses were involved. Fortunately, Roses in May was clean and both he and Saratoga County passed muster during the quarantine period.

The flight progressed on schedule with a stop in England along the way. Allison made good use of her sleeping bag, in between play visits with her horse, while Louie never left Saratoga's side. When the horse landed in Dubai and the doors opened, they were engulfed in a sea of white robes and chattering reporters. More greeted them as they came down the ramp, including hundreds of flash bulbs. It helped to be traveling with Roses in May, the projected star of the show. As usual, Saratoga County was relegated to a walk-on role, but it didn't bother him. Allison was amazed by all the fuss. Not much of it was pointed in her direction. In fact, the Arab newsmen seemed to look right through her as she walked by, leading her horse.

When the van reached his new home, Saratoga County got a glimpse of horse paradise. The stall was easily three times the size he was used to. He had his own air conditioner and supply of bottled water, and best of all, there was his ball and good old orange highway cone.

He paced the depth of his stall, calculating the run he had to the door for his attack strategy. He had a problem. The stall door opening was too high. He could get his head over it, but his long neck would be of no use to him. People reached in and tried to pet him. He could get to their sleeves, but the more important parts of their clothing were out of reach (grabbng those white robes would have been a real hoot).

Allison did not ride him until after the quarantine period of several days ended. Once on the track, Saratoga County readily took to the surface although he was not satisfied doing slow, easy jogs. He was there to run. George had worked him into shape before they left and Allison was tasked with the fine tuning. She was to get him prepared for night racing and the different sights and sounds of Nad al Sheba. There were sights to get prepared for. The track was oddly configured. The turns came late and fast and the horses got the feeling they were headed into the grandstand. Of course, there was also that sea of white garments.

Saratoga wanted to run. His early morning laziness was gone Running was on his mind and fast running at that. Following instructions, Allison kept him in check.

He was fooling around in the saddling paddock one morning, practicing for the big day, when he remembered his old strip the shoe off his hoof trick. Allison was not pleased. In fact, it was the subject of one of her nightly calls to George Weaver. It was a good thing Evelyn and I didn't choose to come, because it allowed George to invite his brother and his farrier, as substitute travelers. This, of course, was perfect for Saratoga County. As in the stakes races last year, at Gulfstream, he was able to gather a friendly solicitous crew around him by the simple act of taking off a shoe.

When George arrived, he proceeded to absorb the sights and sounds of the area (trying to catch up with his horse). He visited the various pre-race activities, including a lavish party in the desert. Not many people knew anything about his horse. They had heard of Pico Central and knew he was the sure winner of the Golden Shaheen, but Saratoga County wasn't particularly familiar. George was resolute in his prediction that his horse had a good chance, but who would listen to a trainer who seemed so young and inexperienced. (He was tall though.)

Race day was hectic. Saratoga County, normally a calm, cool, and collected dude, was spooking a bit. "He never does that," said Allison, "but I must admit I was spooked myself." Coming out of a dark tunnel, into the brilliant lights on the track with tens of thousands of people, all dressed in white, all pressing inward, must have been quite an experience. Saratoga reared up on his hind legs and started backing up, causing the ever present farrier to move the crowd out of the

140

way. (I wonder if our liability policy reaches to the United Arab Emirates.)

After the initial shock wore off, Saratoga started warming to the situation. To him, this was all very interesting. George had some trouble tacking up because Saratoga wanted to see everything going on. When the horses started heading for the track, Allison was trapped in the saddling paddock by the milling crowd, so she stayed to watch the race on the big screen television. Her problem reminded us of being trapped in the crowd at the Melbourne Cup in Australia. The difference, of course, is that Allison's crowd was non-alcoholic.

Allison had run the horse over the track in the morning, so he had some idea what he was getting himself into. The six-furlong track at Nab al Sheba was a straightaway, not the one turn he was used to. It's tough to break old habits such as bearing left in anticipation of the turn. In any event, Saratoga County broke cleanly and set up shop with a group of horses on the left rail, while the others began their running on the right side near the grandstand. Initially trapped behind horses, Javier Castellano pulled his horse to the center of the track and took off.

No matter how the track was configured, Saratoga County knew where the finish line was, and he was heading there. Finally released from the restraints Allison had held him under for two weeks, he unleashed his powerful strides. After he cleared the horses on his left, he headed for the rail, where his instincts told him to go. In the process, he brushed My Cousin Matt, who, in turn, caused Pico Central to check. It was apparent to us watching from Florida, that he had both horses well beaten. When Evelyn checked in from the bathroom, I told her to get out in front of the television set and watch her horse win a $2-million race.

Saratoga County finished the race in 1:11.21 and pulled up reluctantly. After all, this was the first good run he had in weeks. As usual, he slowed down when he knew he had the race won (good old Saratoga, no wasted energy). Had he been able to see the horses closing on the far right, he would have clocked in a better time.

Back in Palm Meadows, a large number of grooms, exercise riders, and trainers gathered, watched the race, and erupted. Allison, still trapped in the saddling paddock, started shouting and jumping up and down. She attracted a crowd of white robed reporters and cameramen who decided she had something to do with the winner (probably the first time they even looked at her). "That was nerve-racking," she told Castellano. "We couldn't find you and figured we got beat." "Look here, look right here, we did it," replied Javier as he hugged Allison on the way to the winner's circle.

TVG caught George Weaver running with his brother and the farrier toward the winner's circle. "I couldn't see down the lane," Weaver said afterwards. "I thought we had it won and then I thought we lost it. When I saw the last eighth of a mile, I knew we had it. He's a lovely horse. He deserves the win," George said, displaying pure emotion.

Pure emotion was on display in our house as well. We were watching TVG playing repeated views of the possible interference. They were of a mind that it didn't affect the outcome of the race. We agreed, but waited anxiously for the race to become official. As TVG was about to go to commercial, they flashed up the official sign. Breathing a sigh of relief, I scraped Evelyn down off the ceiling. After a lengthy run of commercials, TVG returned to the track, and what to our wondering eyes did appear (not a sleigh full of toys and eight tiny reindeer), but a room full of suits, two jockeys, and a television set.

Evelyn got back up on the ceiling and I was frozen to the set, awaiting our fate. In the winner's circle, George Weaver and Allison had no idea what was going on. There was a delay, but no one told them why (add one point for watching from home).

The objection was disallowed, but we didn't know for sure until the meeting broke up and Solis, Pico Central's jockey, said, in response to a reporter's question, "I'm not happy." (He may not have been, but we sure were.) Solis also commented after the race that his horse never got a hold of the track and was beaten fair and square. K.T. Donovan, writing in the *Thoroughbred Times* captured the emotion the best when she wrote, "Weaver kept turning in circles in the winner's circle, unable to calm down. 'I got to say it doesn't get much better than this,' Weaver said, surveying the more than 50,000 fans, who now knew what he had known all along about Saratoga County."

A few of those 50,000 fans stayed around to watch Saratoga cool down. They included ten Japanese horsemen (with money hanging out of their pockets) and several equally as rich looking Irish guys. Allison worried about losing her buddy right on the spot. Her fears were unfounded. The international market tends to look for horses that can run the classic distance, rather than sprinters. It is us Americans who love the instant gratification of the shorter races.

Allison flew back with George Weaver and company on a commercial jet. Saratoga County and Louie, his groom, were left to find their way home a week later. Awaiting him was the horse's most important race, the race for his life.

26

Stallion Duty

At this point, Evelyn and I were drifting on cloud nine. We were still down in Florida, awaiting my second hip operation. I finished the prep work for it, visiting blood banks and general practitioners, and especially, the carpenter who was going to do the sawing and hammering, but the Dubai race was still foremost in my mind. It was a great diversion, because I went through this before and knew what a pain the whole procedure could be. I carried our press clippings with me and described the race to whomever would listen. Over half the fun in the horse business is bragging about your successes. (You never talk about the failures.)

The local off-track betting channel in Saratoga Springs did a nice telephone interview with Evelyn and me. They showed the win picture from the Mr. Prospector every time we spoke. It gave us the opportunity to watch Evelyn and Pauly Walnuts over and over again. They also asked me to narrate the race as they showed it on the screen. Not being able to see their tape, I was lucky to finish my pithy comments just as the race ended. (It must have been the hundred times we played the TVG tape for ourselves previously.)

The questions thrown our way during the interview included: "Where does the horse go from here? Which races are you pointing for? When will Saratoga go to stud and where?" From our standpoint, being asked "when" was much better than being asked "if." In that regard, we had three serious offers. Each differed in some respects, but all hovered around the same number with the ability to retain a percentage ownership if we wished. This was an important consideration, because half the fun of owning a world-class horse is to watch it grow in stature as his progeny begin racing. It can work the other way, of course, and many owners with dreams of Storm Cat ($500,000 stud fee) in their head have ended up with a minor player in a big market.

The mechanics of standing a stallion at stud are fascinating and quite different from those of thoroughbred racing. Operating a broodmare farm in Ocala exposed us to the stallion selection process. Our choices, at that time, ranged from a $20,000 stud fee to a complimentary breeding to a new, unproven stallion. The $20,000 figure was a top amount for Ocala, because the more popular sires go to Kentucky where they can command higher stud fees and draw from a national and international inventory of broodmares. The new stallions without strong pedigrees or big track winnings are offered at a low price, in hopes of building a reputation on the performance of their progeny.

Many farms will gather their own broodmare band and breed their new stallions to them. Our neighbor purchased a number of cheap mares in Ohio and bred them, along with our mare, Ballet Rouge, to Theatre Critic. Although Ballet Critic was a happy result of that breeding (at least happy for us), breeding cheap mares to cheap stallions usually produces cheap racehorses.

When searching for a good stallion to breed to a good broodmare, the process is very similar to examining the catalogues at the horse auctions. Pedigree is important, and in our hurry-up world, a sire who produces two-year-old winners could do the same for you. Grass pedigrees are an issue as well. We bred Ballet Rouge to Theatre Critic precisely for that reason. We wanted, and we got, a grass horse. Distance is a consideration. If the pedigree cries out classic distance, breeders will bring their mares with an eye to the Kentucky Derby

Once a stallion produces a large number of black-type winners, his stud fee skyrockets. If he is a Florida sire, he soon finds himself in Kentucky. Another aspect of breeding shed success is the effect it has on the future sire value of his babies. As an example, sons and daughters of Mr. Prospector or Storm Cat get a lot of takers when they go to stud, even if their racing record is weak or non-existent.

In addition to pedigree, the performance of the stallion during his racing campaign continues to carry weight. Did he win graded stakes races? What were the grades? Were any of them two-year-old stakes? How much purse money did he collect? All good questions. They help to set the price a stud farm is willing to pay for your horse.

In the case of Saratoga County, his pedigree was iffy. Valid Expectations, his sire, had produced average to good runners, with none of them setting the world on fire, at least until Saratoga County arrived. Valid Appeal, the sire of Valid Expectations, was a good, solid stallion who produced tough, consistent runners. He was standing in Florida and recently retired from stud duty, eliminating his line in that state. Standing a new Valid Appeal stallion in Florida, where he was still popular, was a plus. Valid Expectations was standing in Texas and was not readily available to Florida mare owners.

On the performance side, Saratoga's three stakes wins, especially his win in Dubai, were a big boost. He had a win as a two-year-old, but it was a claiming race. That was a bit of a negative. The most significant item on his resume, however, was his total earnings. He was a millionaire, winning almost $1.7-million during his short career. Saratoga was a sprinter and that limited the bidding to domestic stud farms. In total, he presented an attractive package with a good chance of increasing his value if he could replicate himself.

The negotiations came down to the shared ownership conditions. Two of our three offers involved syndicating the horse with our ownership in the form of shares that we could use or sell as we wished. The Vinery stallion station offered a straight percentage ownership, with us contributing 20 percent of the expenses and collecting 20 percent of the revenue. We could sell our ownership if the horse was syndicated down the road (hopefully at an increased value). In addition, the Vinery planned to stand the horse in Florida and we could visit him on a regular basis. For Evelyn, it was not about the money, it was about the horse she had fallen in love with.

The money, especially the purse amount, was important to a number of people. It was a financial windfall for George and Cindy at a key point in their budding careers. For Allison, it was a down payment on a house; for Louie, it meant a trip back to Mexico to visit his mother; for Castellano, it was a good bump in his yearly earnings; and for us, the purse plus the pending sales proceeds allowed the Pollards to finally break even after twenty years of losses in the business. Another way to look at it was we finally got back the money we spent on the first lousy horse Buddy Leroux talked us into buying.

The reason for all this financial and emotional celebration was standing patiently in his stall at Nab al Sheba, wondering where everybody went. Louie was still with him, as was his ball and his orange highway cone, but it wasn't any fun anymore. No people to disrobe, no little Benjamin to grab, and most of all, very little exercise. In other words, he wasn't getting out much anymore, and he resented it. "Where were Allison and the tall guy? What a bunch of ingrates," he must have thought.

Fortunately they weren't there long. Saratoga and Louie were soon winging back in the big plane, but without female companionship. With no one to play with, it was kind of boring. His return was interrupted by several quarantine days in upstate New York. Unfortunately, because infection was still circulating around the barns, he could not ship to Belmont. Saratoga County was put in a confining stall with little light. It was certainly not the digs he had in Dubai. To make matters worse, Louie was not allowed to see him during that period. The effect on a party animal like Saratoga County was devastating. He got more depressed and more lethargic as time went on.

We were really concerned. Especially Evelyn, who hated to have her friend locked up in a prison cell. From my standpoint (being a money-grubbing ex-banker), I was concerned that the newly inked contract with the Vinery could not be completed until he was checked over by the insurance company doctors and found to be healthy and potentially virile. (The policy insured mortality and reproductive ability.)

Upon his release from detention, we shipped him right to a local clinic so we could determine whether his depression was medical, mental, or both. After a number of days there and the return of Louie, Saratoga County perked up. He passed his physical with the insurance company and Evelyn and I breathed a sigh of relief. The relief proved to be short-lived.

27

Aftereffects

The coverage of Saratoga County's exploits in the Middle East was better on a worldwide basis than it was here in the United States, but we were content he had accomplished things that very few horses ever had. The purse money took a slow trip from Dubai. We had already made plans for it, following the typical horse owner's strategy of reinvesting in new stock (a strategy designed to keep them broke). Getting pictures out of Dubai, especially win pictures, was a real challenge. Although we eventually got a win picture of sorts, it didn't live up to United States standards.

Win pictures are an interesting subject. The photographer is always present in the winner's circle, asking the all-important question, "How many copies do you want?" You are forced to scan the assembled crowd and make a quick decision, weighing hurt feelings against the cost involved. I'm sure you are thinking, "You just won a purse. Why be so cheap about it?" (That's what the photographer thinks as well when he offers you no quantity discount.)

In our early racing days at Rockingham Park, the cost of the win pictures began challenging the purse amount (minus the cost of the ice). When we couldn't attend the race, we usually made the quantity decision in advance. It always amazed us how many people we didn't know appeared in the win picture with our horses. In fact, many of them looked more like owners than we did. (I'm speaking about myself, not Evelyn.) And certainly those people were never around in the pre-dawn hours when the unglamorous part of racing occurs.

Everyone displays their win pictures differently. We decided early on to put the pictures in black metal certificate frames and hang them in our two houses. We started, as did Buddy Leroux, with big rooms and very small displays of Thoroughbred successes. Whereas Buddy's collection didn't grow much over the years, ours did. We now have sixty-three pictures in each location (helped by all those cheap Rockingham Park and Suffolk Downs wins). Over the years, the manufacturers stopped making the black metal certificate frames, leaving us to scour the stores and pick up a supply when we could find them. I discovered the fastest way to start a losing streak was to happen upon a large supply of frames. (Who says I'm not superstitious?)

Speaking about superstition, George Weaver would leave front bandages on Saratoga County, even if the horse had no need for them. As I mentioned earlier, Allison Logan was assigned to exercise all our horses. Trainers will never change a horse's stall as long as the horse is winning. During a winning streak, owners and trainers won't change their clothes (one might say, you can smell a winning streak). We consider it unlucky to bet on our own runners. Other owners do just the opposite. One of our reasons for not going to Dubai was the much better win percentage we had watching at home on television rather than being there. Evelyn can tell you conclusively numbers three and four are lucky for our horses. (I suspect that a study of post positions might prove her right.) In any event, Saratoga County won the Golden Shaheen from the eighth post, although on a straight track.

The naming game, discussed earlier, also encompasses a good deal of superstition. Saratoga County's arrival early in our relationship with George Weaver, led us to start naming all our horses after counties. In the same manner, our first graded stakes winner, Kachemak Bay, unleashed a flood of horses named after bays. Although the lucky name strategy hasn't guaranteed success, it has made picking names easier, and produced fairly good runners. Pelham Bay, selected and trained by Pat Kelly, is a stakes winner and a good number of counties have found the finish line first.

The original county, Saratoga, was getting back into shape and seemed none the worse for his globe-hopping experience. The deal we made with the Vinery was for us to continue owning and running the horse until after the Breeders' Cup races. Official ownership would not pass until November and George Weaver would continue to schedule his races. We would continue to pay the bills. They had purchased Saratoga's breeding rights and insured him against any mishaps.

We felt we had the best sprinter in the world. He was unbeaten in 2005 with three graded stakes wins and $1,380,000 in total earnings. At that point, no other sprinter in the country could match his 2005 performance. The various polls and rankings put him in fourth or fifth position, but now he was moving up. Defeating horses like Don Six and Pico Central, who had been ranked above him, aided the process. The one horse still ranked above Saratoga was the undefeated fan favorite Lost in the Fog, who had yet to meet a horse with the class and character of our horse. Our ultimate goal for Saratoga County was the Eclipse Award, given to the country's best sprinter of 2005. The award is determined by the vote of the racing press and is based on performance in the year just passed. The honor is the equine equivalent of the Academy Award.

Weaver's strategy was to point for the Breeders' Cup Sprint and our chance to look Lost in the Fog in the eye and finally prove who was the better horse. The race could be preceded by a sprint at Belmont, or a stakes race at Saratoga. George felt his horse would tell him when he was ready to run.

Saratoga County felt he was ready to run right now. The whole Dubai experience was rapidly fading from his mind. As he did with most issues, Saratoga tended to forget the spooky stuff and only remember the pleasant things that happened over there. He thought the racetrack crowd was a bit over the top, and he didn't care much for the sea of white he was confronted with. The stall was great but not very good for biting. Allison and Louie were always there, and the track really felt good under his feet. He'd be looking for a similar surface here in this country, but wasn't too sure he'd find one.

He had initially felt abandoned on his trip home, but he forgave everyone involved. He was back now basking in the glory of his accomplishments. The assistant trainer at Belmont (Allison was still in Florida) took him out each morning and rode with great pride. The other horses had heard tell of his exploits and were looking at him with a newfound respect. Even the fillies were seeing him in a different light. Maybe he was going to handle those rumored stud duties after all. The tall guy seemed to be spending more and more time with him. "Didn't he have other horses to deal with?" Saratoga County must have thought.

Weaver did have other horses to deal with and some of them were ours. The Saratoga meet was rapidly approaching and he had a batch of two-year-olds to get ready. The hallmark of the Saratoga meet was its two-year-old races. The timing of these races was not ideal, because it's a little early for them. Trainers like Todd Pletcher with a large supply of young horses can always find a small percentage mature enough to run early. Trainers with only a few youngsters are under pressure to run them, even though their best races may not happen until the fall and winter months. Add to the mix, the insatiable desire of the owners to see their expensive babies run at the prestigious Saratoga meet. The result of all this is a real pain in the neck for the trainer. George Weaver was not exempted, even though he had just won the richest sprint in the world.

28

The Illness

In the Trainer Speak section, I reviewed the various ways trainers pass on bad news to their owners. They do so gradually if the horse is in his stall with no visible problems, and has the possibility of recovering with little intervention. They give out enough information so if the horse turns for the worse, the owner must admit he had been told about the problem. "Remember I told you," is the trainer's usual response. This approach was clearly not appropriate when George Weaver had to tell us about Saratoga County's sudden illness.

Several horses in the Weaver barn had come down with throat problems and the vet checked out several ways to combat it. After discussions with several knowledgeable sources, they started an antibiotic regimen that would last several days. The illness was not serious and the medicine was neither uncommon nor dangerous, yet halfway through the oral applications, the three horses being treated became extremely sick. They all started displaying colic symptoms at the same time. The vet shipped them to several clinics depending on the apparent degree of illness. The one who looked to be in the worst shape, a well-bred filly who had won her first two races, was sent to the renowned Cornell University Veterinary Clinic. Saratoga County and a young, not very successful, filly, were vanned to a smaller clinic near the racetrack.

The horses began their stay at the clinic on June 8 showing depression, mild fever, and an elevated heart and respiratory rate. A presumptive diagnosis of colitis was made and they began therapy on both horses. (We had no idea what all this meant.) On June 10, they both started showing evidence of lameness, attributed to laminitis. George Weaver's initial hope that Saratoga County, who seemed to be the least affected of the three horses, would survive and recover were dashed by the findings of an expert, whom we flew in from Texas.

William Moyer was a professor and head of the Large Animal Medicine and Surgery Department at Texas A&M University. He was one of the country's foremost experts on laminitis and he summed up his examination as follows. "The colt, on my day of examination, is showing considerable lameness involving all four limbs; and it is important to point out that he is also on appropriate anti-inflammatory medications to help control pain. The distal displacement (sinking) of the coffin bones clearly demonstrates massive cellular damage. Based on my experience, the degree of structural damage will increase. The structural damage I anticipate will involve further displacement and secondary coffin bone involvement as the result of avascular necrosis. It is my opinion the colt meets the criteria for humane euthanasia."

In more direct terms, a horse with acute laminitis can look forward to having his large leg bones sink through the spongy shock absorber material and come out into the hoof. The hoof, in a sense, falls off. Fortunately, the horse is not aware of what is happening and is usually euthanized before the pain gets too bad. Unfortunately, no controlled studies exist to indicate what is the best management regimen for the horse. In other words, once laminitis proceeds as far and as quickly as it had with Saratoga County, the best that could be expected was to stabilize him and mask the pain. Recovery was no longer an option. In light of these facts, the unaccomplished filly was euthanized, but too many people were in love with Saratoga County to allow for any quick decision.

Saratoga's plight brought all the fringe experts on laminitis out of the woodwork. George, refusing to leave any stone unturned, studied each suggested cure as it appeared. One suggestion was a procedure that involved cutting off all four hooves, putting the horse in a sling mechanism, swimming him for exercise and letting the feet regrow. Apparently, this approach had been successful once, although it was a lengthy and uncomfortable treatment. Subsequent attempts to duplicate the success failed, and in one case, the horse's feet grew in backwards. Experts in the field believe it is unethical for veterinarians or farriers to say to owners that "had someone instituted a particular therapy at a particular time in the course of the disease, the horse could have had a better outcome." No viable solution seemed to be available, but George Weaver wouldn't give up.

Evelyn and Allison set up a vigil at the clinic. It was in a convenient spot so it was easy for them to spend part of each day with their horse. Evelyn bought an endless supply of carrots and Allison made sure his stall was in top shape and his ball and cone were on hand. Saratoga had an outside stall and could see cars pulling up. His response to the women was always cheerful. The doctors and assistants at the clinic fell in love with him, and although they knew better medically, they were ready to defend him against being euthanized. We gave them copies of his win pictures and his press clippings to hang in the barn and offices. He was not only lovable, he was famous.

From Saratoga County's point of view, these remained interesting times. The sore throat had bothered him, but the cure seemed worse than the disease. It knocked him off his pins for a while, but he was feeling better and he was certainly being fussed over. It was sort of like his detention period after his return from Dubai, but now he had company. The tall guy visited him a lot, although he didn't seem as happy as he usually did. Of course, Allison and the cute little owner were always upbeat. His supply of carrots seemed endless, but he would have liked more exercise.

One day a mare and her foal were being loaded onto a van in the parking lot and the feeling she invoked in Saratoga was a reminder of the stallion duty in the wings. He let out a whoop, which for some reason seemed to bother the cute little owner, who was there at the time. Although he seemed to be getting back to his old self, his feet were really bothering him. He couldn't seem to find a comfortable position in which to stand. After Allison spread a thick layer of sand in his stall, he felt a lot better. "It was sort of like the track in Dubai," he must have mused.

I couldn't keep Evelyn away. Her visits became twice a day, and she started bringing her dog along. Saratoga County became more and more dependent on her visits and would shoo away anyone at his stall door when she arrived. Evelyn recalled a clinical assistant talking to him one day when she pulled up. Saratoga took a mouthful of water and sprayed it all over the unsuspecting interloper. She got the message and left, much to Evelyn's embarrassment. (As usual, Saratoga County got what he wanted.)

Although everyone knew what the horse's future held, no one would admit it. I was worried they would allow too much pain before they put him down. He had good days and he had bad days and everyone was looking for a miracle. It never came. Saratoga County got steadily worse. His bones continued to sink and rotate. He was down more than he was up, and Evelyn spent more and more time with him. One evening, she and her dog lay on the floor with her horse, and her dog kissed him.

157

It was the last chat they ever had. The next day, the vets decided Saratoga's time had come. Evelyn didn't see him again. She wanted to retain the last image of her favorite animals together.

Because a large insurance settlement was involved, the horse had to be euthanized at Cornell. They managed to get Saratoga County up, fill him with painkillers, brush and shine his coat, and load him onto a van. George Weaver arrived just at that moment. It was really harder for him to see his horse looking so good, as opposed to the way Evelyn had seen him the night before. George's knees buckled and his only thought was his horse looked too good to die.

When you get to live to a ripe old age, one of the negatives is that you attend a lot of funerals. I can't remember ever being quite as sad and grateful as we were with Saratoga County. Sad because this wonderful animal had been as close to us as any family member, something we don't recommend for other new owners. (But he was so darn special.) Grateful because he did so much for so many people. He rewarded Evelyn and me for years of dedication to the horse business. He jump-started the careers of George and Cindy Weaver, not to mention Allison and Louie. He also rewarded the thousands of people who just enjoyed watching him run.

We debated what to do with Saratoga's remains. The normal disposition had no appeal for us and we didn't have the land for a burial scenario. Evelyn hit on the cremation option, and fortunately, Cornell had the capacity to handle a horse. We knew the whole process would be a sad one, but it seemed appropriate. We had a friend visiting from Kentucky and she helped to diffuse some of the pain Evelyn was feeling while we waited for the vet to hand-deliver the ashes. Our discussion encompassed the potential size of a horse's ashes and how we might eventually dispose of them. (I've discovered that busy discussions tend to mask the pain of sad situations.)

The ashes were quite heavy, as you might suspect, and the mahogany box they were in resembled a small coffin. I knew right then and there the ashes weren't going anywhere. They would remain with Evelyn for the rest of her life. Even a hard-hearted ex-banker like myself had to agree with her plan.

Several weeks later, we had an Irish wake at our house that centered around Saratoga County's life and accomplishments. Evelyn invited family, friends, and various people we met at the track over the years. It tested the parking capacity of our property. When we bought the house, part of the sales pitch was the number of cars it could hold. I threatened to go back to selling parking spaces during the racing season many times since then. (Watching Evelyn park cars would be the best part.)

The gathering went well. Evelyn brought a favored few over to the miniature casket next to her piano. She had been composing appropriate tunes for her horse. When it came time for the toast, she brought tears to everyone's eyes.

"To Saratoga County," she said. "I'm sure he's up in heaven running freely across the fields. Happy. Because his feet no longer hurt." She had previously broken up our tough New York City lawyer with the same speech.

29

Lawyers

During Saratoga County's illness and subsequent death, the blame game was played at a very subdued level. It was clear to everyone involved that some serious mistakes had been made and these wonderful animals had been innocent victims. Our vet had the presence of mind to immediately confiscate and lock up the unused syringes of the medicine he had been giving the horses. He also notified the pharmaceutical company that something was very, very wrong. A syringe was sent to Cornell for testing and they indicated that the antibiotic involved appeared to be mixed at a higher-than-specified strength.

We contacted a New York City law firm with experience in cases such as ours. The lawyer we used had experience from the side of the corporations defending themselves against litigant claims. We figured he understood the process. A lawsuit was filed at the beginning of October, 2005 by four owners alleging a defective antibiotic product caused the death of three animals and the severe damage to a fourth.

In addition to the horses in the Weaver barn, a horse named Egghead was treated at Belmont Park for a cut over one of his hocks with the same product from the same company. Egghead developed the same symptoms as Weaver's horses, contracted laminitis, and was put down on July 11. The irony here was Egghead's status as a racehorse. He was a sprinter, well-regarded in his division, and the only horse to have given the celebrated Lost in the Fog a run for his money. With the latter horse ranked above us in the standings, we were awaiting their next matchup with interest. Egghead was scratched and the face-off never occurred. Now we knew why.

The lawsuit went on to say the horses, staying at Saratoga Race Course, had contracted a laryngeal infection on June 8 and a veterinarian administered a chloramphenicol palmitate product to Yankee Penny, Cathy's Choice, and Saratoga County. The treatment came less than three weeks before the start of the 137th annual racing season at Saratoga Springs. Within hours of being injected with the antibiotic, the health of the horses deteriorated. The suit further alleged the medicine was defective in its design, manufacture, compounding, mixing, formulating, or labeling. The product administered as treatment for the four thoroughbred racehorses (including Egghead) instead led to the slow, painful demise of three of the horses.

Yankee Penny, although not as well-known as our horse, had won her first two races as a two-year-old. The owner had been approached to sell her for a sizeable sum and she appeared to be a filly with a big future. Cathy's Choice was owned by friends of ours. She was well-bred and certainly close to their hearts.

The filing was picked up by a local paper and given a good-sized headline. It was only a matter of time before the case would get national attention, driven by the notoriety of Saratoga County. Even after he died, Saratoga continued to battle for respect. His name had not disappeared from the sprinter standings and we were still holding out some slight hope we could get some recognition in the Eclipse Award proceedings.

In the lawsuit the players from the side of the injured horses were many. The insurance company obtained by the Vinery to protect their breeding interest in Saratoga County had issued us a check for 80 percent of the purchase price and taken over our claim against the pharmaceutical company. They became a major litigant at that point. In fact, it was a search of their own records that uncovered the payout to the owners of Egghead. Those owners had assumed, at the time, that their horse reacted badly to an antibiotic and the insurance company agreed. Neither had any suspicion about the quality of the medicine or had it tested. When it turned out to be the same formula from the same company at the same time, the insurance company added some more money to their claim and we had another smoking gun.

The Vinery had its purchase price covered by the insurance, and never took ownership of our horse, but they were still interested in regaining some of the future profits from the horse's projected stud career. They joined the litigation, as did the owners of Yankee Penny who were looking to repay their horse's purchase price and get some compensation for her future as a broodmare. The owners of Cathy's Choice were looking for their purchase price, and everyone wanted to be reimbursed for their medical bills.

We piggybacked on the insurance company's claim looking to get our 20 percent retained ownership amount, which was uninsured. We also joined with the Vinery in their attempt to put a value on the future stud career of Saratoga County. We had no illusions about how much money this would all add up to. The amount didn't concern Evelyn. What she wanted was payback from the pharmaceutical company for taking away her best friend. As she would tell anyone who would listen, "I want their company, their houses, their cars." (And, I assume, their first-born.)

We had hoped the company would settle before the case made it to the thoroughbred media which would put their reputation into question. The public exposure, in the local papers, of our filing eliminated their incentive. The major racing magazines and papers picked up on the story. From this point on the case will surely bog down into long litigation which will produce tests and experts on both sides. It's hard to believe four horses in two places with different medical backgrounds could come down with an identical reaction at the same time; thus, proving our case will be a long, difficult struggle.

30

Respect at Last

Evelyn bridled at the lack of attention afforded her horse. She wrote a letter to the editor of our local Saratoga Springs paper. In it, she expressed her frustration at the poor coverage Saratoga County received in his home town from the press, the local politicians, and the National Museum of Racing. When Funny Cide won the Derby and the Preakness, he received everything short of a brass band, and Mary Lou Whitney's Birdstone, who won the Belmont Stakes, got a street named after him. Saratoga County, the county namesake, with both trainer and owners living in town, was pretty much ignored. As I explained to Evelyn, her horse got no respect before the Gotham, the Mr. Prospector, the General George or the Golden Shaheen. What she had was the Rodney Dangerfield of thoroughbred racing.

Evelyn's letter to the editor received some interesting reactions. Her friends stood behind her efforts to seek recognition for her horse. Others felt she was right, but should not expect much response, especially from the "in" crowd. (Evelyn has never been in anyone's "in" crowd.) We did, however, get a nice response from several of the county officials. Two of the commissioners, "Skip" Scirocco and Phil Klein, contacted us. The former spent time on our front porch, letting us regale him with our horse's exploits.

Skip parked his County Animal Control truck in our driveway and when Evelyn came home from shopping, she blanched white. I figured she thought her dog had either run away, bit the postman, bit me, destroyed the interior of the house, or worse. Her letter got a boost from the proximity of election day, which involved the re-election campaign of the two supervisors.

We were invited to attend the next meeting of the board and responded with Saratoga County's whole family. The group included Evelyn and me, George and Cindy Weaver and their son Ben, and Allison Logan and her friend Tiffany. Supervisor meetings do not seem to attract large crowds, and in this case, the spectators were outnumbered by the supervisors. We added a healthy number to the audience figure. Ben brought his train set and played on the floor between the seats.

Our horse was described as a genuine local hero. The proclamation read, in part:

> **WHEREAS**, it is the privilege and distinct honor of the Board of Supervisors to recognize the outstanding and noteworthy accomplishments of Saratoga County residents; and
>
> **WHEREAS**, Saratoga Springs residents Richard and Evelyn M. Pollard were the proud owners of a four-year-old thoroughbred colt, Saratoga County, who concluded his successful racing career this year with career earnings of $1,646,590; and
>
> **WHEREAS**, Saratoga County posted an impressive career record of six wins, four second place finishes, and one third place finish in seventeen starts; and
>
> **WHEREAS**, Saratoga County won his first race at historic Saratoga Race Course during the 2003 summer meet; and
>
> **WHEREAS**, Saratoga County's career victories included exciting wins in the 2004 Gotham Stakes at Aqueduct, the 2005 Mr. Prospector Handicap at Gulfstream Park in Florida, and the 2005 General George Handicap at Laurel Park in Maryland; and

WHEREAS, on March 26, 2005, Saratoga County traveled across the globe to the United Arab Emirates, and established himself as the best sprinter in the world with his thrilling and convincing win in the $2 million Dubai Golden Shaheen, completing the 1,200 meter race in a time of 1:11.21; now, therefore, it is hereby

PROCLAIMED, that the Saratoga County Board of Supervisors hereby recognizes, honors and expresses its great pride to Richard and Evelyn Pollard on their superb effort and skill in raising, training, owning, managing and racing Saratoga County.

The county supervisor reading the proclamation concluded with the comment that it was clear to him this was more than a horse to the people representing him.

We hoped Skip and Phil would get their reward in heaven and told them so. They didn't get much of a reward down here on earth, because they both got turned out of office in the election. It seems doing the right thing for horse-owning constituents doesn't deliver a lot of votes. From Evelyn's point of view, the letter to the editor was very successful. It didn't get a rise out of the Museum of Racing, but it did produce an invitation to a Board of Supervisors' meeting and a nice proclamation suitable for framing.

Flush with success, Evelyn decided to employ the power of letters to the editor again. She wrote the *Thoroughbred Times* and *The Blood-Horse* asking the racing community to remember a brave and talented horse who never ducked a tough race and beat the best sprinters in the country, while setting a track record at Gulfstream Park.

Her letter probably contributed to Saratoga County's nomination for an Eclipse Award as sprinter of the year. Even though the supervisors' meeting was in close proximity to our house and the trip to California for the Eclipse ceremony was a bit more onerous, we decided to attend. Evelyn, George Weaver, and I were about to take the trip that Saratoga County was smart enough to avoid.

31

Eclipse Awards

The first Eclipse Awards dinner was held at The Waldorf Astoria in New York City on January 26, 1972. It was the consolidation of years of championship awards, in various forms, presented since 1936. Currently, members of three eligible organizations vote on winners in ten divisional categories, which include Saratoga County's sprint division. The three groups are the National Thoroughbred Racing Association, the *Daily Racing Form*, and the National Turf Writers' Association. The same groups also select a horse of the year, an outstanding owner, breeder, trainer, jockey, and apprentice jockey.

We, of course, viewed our horse as the best sprinter of 2005, undefeated in three graded stakes races with earnings far in excess of any horse in his division. We were aware, however, of the lack of respect he has always received, and the fact that he left the scene early in the year. As a result, we were stunned to receive notice of Saratoga County's nomination as an Eclipse finalist.

Evelyn was buoyed by the recognition of her horse. It added to the letters she had been receiving, professing admiration and affection. My job, as always, was to lower her expectations without dashing her hopes.

The other two nominees had more visibility than Saratoga County. Lost in the Fog had won ten straight this past year, without ever facing a horse of Saratoga's class. He did, however, become a media darling with a great deal of hoopla leading up to the Breeder's Cup Sprint, where he finished well off the board. Silver Train won the Breeder's Cup Sprint, usually a launching platform for the Eclipse Award. His performance for the rest of the year was not as noteworthy. (But, in many ways, thoroughbred racing is a "What have you done for me lately?" sport.)

Win, lose, or draw, Saratoga County's family was going to California for the Awards ceremony. It was to be a cameo appearance with Cindy holding down the barn while George made the trip. Evelyn didn't want to leave her new puppy alone for too long, and, not being a fan of flying, I wanted to get the whole trip behind me as soon as possible. Allison Logan, a veteran of long Saratoga County air travel, wasn't about to let us attend without her. I'm sure her horse would have agreed.

We hoped one of the good points of being nominated would be reading about the horse's exploits in the two weeks leading up to the ceremony. Instead, Evelyn searched in vain for at least a mention of her horse in the racing press. The *Thoroughbred Times* did acknowledge that the sprint division was competitive, but the competition was between Lost in the Fog and Silver Train. The *Daily Racing Form* counted eight of the ten individual horse divisions as being "slam dunks," suggesting representatives of those nominees "can start walking up to the stage right now. Your statue awaits."

When Evelyn realized no statue would be awaiting her or Saratoga County in California, she fell into a funk (a sophisticated medical condition). Two of our horses, one running at Gulfstream on Saturday and the other at Aqueduct on Sunday, failed to make it onto the board, and she was not in the best of humor for the long trip west on Monday. The only offset for me was we couldn't get adjoining seats on the crowded flight. As for me, I equipped myself with a portable DVD player and the first two seasons of "Dallas" with the intention of burying myself in the past while I waited for the future.

Although the flight was uneventful, the hotel managed to lose our garment bags in transit between the front door and our room. We spent a couple of hours in the bar musing about how we would handle the dinner without the proper uniforms. I was reminded about the old one-liner that went something like "the world is a tuxedo and I feel like a pair of brown shoes."

Just like Hollywood's finest converge at the Academy Awards, racing's elite flock to the annual Eclipse Awards extravaganza in Beverly Hills. It was fun to watch the various players in the racing business come and go. Chatting with John Velazquez and his wife brought back memories of races gone by. Jockeys who ride a great number of horses over their careers can hardly be expected to remember every horse they ever rode, but ours rang a bell with him. Especially the anxious look on George Weaver's face when he arrived in the winner's circle to see if Saratoga County was claimed out of his first start. Velazquez had ridden him to that blowout finish at Saratoga in that $75,000 maiden claimer.

John also remembered the time the Johnny Campo-trained Kachemak Bay beat King Cugat and Jerry Bailey in the Pilgrim. (I guess when you win a race with a 29–to-1 horse over a 3-to-5 favorite, it tends to stick in your mind.)

We also met the principals of Ashado, the favorite for older female honors. Evelyn tried to get them to give up a few of their first place votes. (As it turned out, we needed a lot more than a few.) Watching the racing world pass by, it struck us how young our trainer is. It's a real feather in his cap to be the trainer of an Eclipse nominee at the ripe old age of thirty-five. We were proud of him.

We headed down the red carpet to immortality (or something like that). Evelyn has this cute little trick she does with her glasses, putting them on when she wants to see where she's walking, and taking them off when someone points a camera at her. She was doing a lot of ons and offs as we approached the cocktail party.

When we were finding our table, Evelyn was in the glasses-off mode, wandering away and running into Bobby Frankel, who directed her to the Weaver table. When Evelyn arrived, all a-twitter about her encounter, I had to point out that he should have been all a-twitter about running in to her. After all, she's a big-time owner and the industry couldn't run without people like her. And, after all, how is she going to get into the in-crowd without acting like an in-crowder?

One of the nicer surprises of the evening was the official program. It featured a full page of hype on each nominee, and did a terrific job of singing our horse's praises while calling people's attention to his tragic death. Had it been in the voters' hands earlier, we might have fared a little better. It was such a great write-up we considered sending it out with our Christmas card (if only to get even with the people who send us their boring life story every year). We had been putting a picture of our best horse on the card, making it a sort of Pollard Eclipse Award.

The ceremony itself was interesting. It had an Oscar flavor to it, with each of the nominees' best race showing up on the big screen before the winner was announced. A camera close-up of each principal was captured as the envelope was opened and the winner disclosed. For some reason (probably male chauvinism) they had my picture up there instead of Evelyn's. At that moment, she was in a glasses-off mode and I vowed never to tell her. Having this little bit of exposure, I played with the idea of making an obscene gesture when the winner was announced, but decided no one would think it was funny (and it wouldn't do much for Evelyn's in-crowd status).

In the final analysis, we got eleven first place votes to Silver Train's thirty, and Lost in the Fog's 209. (Eleven brave and intelligent people.)

The evening made us glad we had come and content in the knowledge we had chosen the right industry. The legends were there—Ogden Phipps and Penny Chenery of Secretariat fame on the owner's side and Gary Stevens, Chris McCarron, and the retiring Jerry Bailey representing the legendary jockeys. Old favorites were still winning races and winning awards, while budding superstars like Todd Pletcher and his protégé George Weaver were making their mark in history. We came away proud to be in their company.

32

New Season—New Tattoo

It's human nature, but not very nice, to root against your horses after they are claimed or after you sell them at auction. Their failure puts a happier face on your position. We discovered the same holds true for the Eclipse Awards. Since Saratoga County was pretty much ignored by the voters, we were anxious to see our position enhanced by the future performance of the horses who received more votes.

Silver Train had a slow start in '06, but produced a credible record with two wins and a second out of five races and $473 million in earnings through October. Lost in the Fog, the convincing winner of the Eclipse Sprint Division, suffered a different fate, one that was quite distressing. It, in fact, reminded us so much of Saratoga's that it affected us deeply. He contracted cancer and had to be euthanized.

Evelyn's reaction was true to form. She figured her horse had been biding his time in horse heaven awaiting the arrival of his prime adversary, just as he had been waiting patiently to take on Don Six and Pico Central with their folios of press clippings. She could envision the two horses charging through the clouds, locked in a match race, decided by a stirring stretch run. It would be a proper culmination of Saratoga County's outstanding career. She was sure of the outcome.

While I was still playing the "What if?" game, Evelyn decided to take another step toward immortalizing her horse.

A tattoo always seemed to be a man thing. At least it was fifty years ago when I got mine (a beer glass with the words "The Old Sarge" scrolled beneath). My motivation, at the time, was clear and heroic. My younger brother, who was training to be a pilot in the United States Air Force, had crashed his plane in Moultrie, Georgia and died. The day after his funeral, I found myself on the back pavilion of the town beach intent on drowning my sorrows. I was joined by three guys I'd never met before and we were soon toasting my brother (aka The Old Sarge). After an afternoon of stacking empty beer cans, my leadership qualities began to surface and I led the group to Rockaway Playland where we reinforced my brother's memory by getting matching tattoos.

We never met each other again; but years later, I passed a rather overweight guy on the beach, bathing in the sun, surrounded by a large family. He sported a tattoo that read, "The Old Sarge." I hustled on by, covering my arm, fearing he hadn't been too happy about my leadership skills when he sobered up.

Evelyn's desire to immortalize her horse on decorated skin was fueled by a recent female fad. Tattoos are now viewed as fashion accessories and can be found anywhere on the body. I reminded her of the story about my brother and emphasized the permanence of her decision as well as the problem some people might have with it.

As an example, I recalled the first time we invited the CEO of my Boston bank to our lakeside home in New Hampshire. It was a sunny day and I refused to cover up my arm for a stodgy New England banker. He didn't comment on "The Old Sarge," but his eyes showed his thoughts. "Why did I hire this guy? Just look at his arm—he's common—he won't make it in proper society."

As it turned out, I did make it well enough to afford a bunch of horses for Evelyn, including one good enough to get inked on her leg.

We went to the Cool Cat tattoo parlor and met Kevin (who was doing a good Elvis impersonation). He copied Saratoga's Dubai win picture and did an outstanding job. Evelyn kept a stiff upper lip during the process, proving that her threshold for pain is directly related to the goal she has in mind (she can't stand having her teeth cleaned).

For my part, watching a bunch of young women getting decorated on all parts of their bodies was quite engrossing and I told Evelyn to take her time and get the job done right!

The result was just great. Rather than a generic horse's head, the tattoo actually looked like Saratoga County right down to his wild eye, his white bridle, and his hood with George Weaver's initials on display. I guess this means we're stuck with George for life (a tactical error when dealing with a trainer).

33

It's Not Over Yet

We often look back on our lives in the business from the days when our first horse, Shot Gun Evie, was running at Suffolk Downs and providing us with a good deal of entertainment and pride. Just picking up the *Daily Racing Form* and reading about our entry was such a thrill in those days.

Twenty years have passed and almost 100 horses have come in and out of our lives. Almost all of them have cost us money—some more, some less. Saratoga County managed, in his short career, to break us even financially, so we are, in a sense, starting all over again. That's pretty much what the business is all about. Beginnings and endings.

Some horses live to a ripe old age and have happy, productive lives. Most, however, are only around for a short period. Their fragile physical makeup comes under siege daily from sloppy dirt tracks, dangerous turf, a variety of diseases, unhealthy attempts to push immature runners, and unfortunate programs to pump up horses before a sale.

Because so much of the business is out of the hands of the owners and their trainers, they find themselves turning to superstition, and sometimes, religion. It is, after all, an undertaking with high odds against success. Evelyn and I would never participate in other gambling enterprises with such little chance of getting our money back.

Thoroughbred racing is really about something else. It's about hope. My favorite saying is still "high hopes and low expectations." Owners who keep that in mind seem to enjoy themselves at all levels of cost and competition. Each year, every new yearling or two-year-old arriving at the barn carries the possibility of the Triple Crown, the World Cup races, or the Eclipse Awards. There is a saying in the business that no owner ever committed suicide with an unraced two-year old in the barn.

We seem to have held our own, and when we think about why, several things come to mind:

Luck—Evelyn was always a great believer in the power of numbers. She once named a horse Lyn's Trinity because her hip number, when she was purchased, was 333, and she claimed to have awoken one night to see her bedroom digital clock flashing the time at 3:33. (As you probably already guessed, Lyn's Trinity didn't win many races.) Evelyn also discovered that good things happened on the 23rd of the month. She was born on that day in February, as was her current dog. George Weaver was born on the 23rd as was his son. Our son, David, was also born on the 23rd as was my mother. Many of our horses won their races on the 23rd, and finally, the Eclipse Awards, to which Saratoga County had been nominated, took place on the 23rd. I didn't put my money on Saratoga winning the sprint title (it was a contest between Evelyn's numerical omen and the horse's Rodney Dangerfield complex). It wasn't much of a contest. I do believe, however, luck has been a part of our success (or lack of failure).

Religion—Evelyn has long talks with God, almost every night as long as I've known her (mostly to give her the strength to put up with me). She swears many of the good things happening to us were the direct result of those conversations. Somewhere along the way, George Weaver signed on to her approach, and provided the press with some great quotes about the "the man upstairs." We also found George looking upward a lot more than usual. As you recall, when Scott Lake said it would take an act of God to beat Don Six in the General George, Weaver really believed he had gotten one of those acts. Still, the death of Saratoga County took a fairly big toll on the faith of both Evelyn and George. The question of why bad things happen to good people (or good horses) has been debated by theologians since the beginning of time.

Hard work—Being an owner is not to be taken lightly. The IRS, trying to reduce the write-offs taken by owners against other income, has set up a complex series of rules to be followed when an owner is claiming hands-on management. We have always felt leaving your fate to your trainer or purchasing agent is not the way to increase your probability of success. As I've tried to explain in this book, it's important to have a first-hand knowledge of the racing business and an awareness of what's happening to your horses and your money. Owners have the ultimate say about their racing experience and changing trainers is always an option. They should be willing to roll up their sleeves and get personally involved.

We hope this book helps.

Epilogue

Consigned by Classic Bloodstock and assigned hip number 769, the big, chestnut colt by Sweetsouthernsaint, out of the Two Punch mare, Blazing Punch, looked like any of the other horses in the April Ocala Breeders sale of two-year-olds in training. The sale boasted no big-time prospects (the highest purchase price turned out to be only $375,000).

We were following the sale up in Saratoga Springs and George was doing his usual act, going from barn to barn trying to find the proverbial diamond in the rough. It appeared he might have found it when he called to tell us he "really, really" liked hip number 769.

The bidding for George's choice broke through the bargain level in about an instant and didn't look like it was going to stop. It did, at $250,000, the fourth highest price of the sale. George Weaver stayed in all the way and a new, big-time horse joined our barn.

There was something about the way he arrived at his new digs that seemed kind of familiar. Hip number 769 looked over at the welcoming group and appeared satisfied they were nice enough. The tall guy, who kept bidding on him with grim determination, was there, as was an exercise rider named Allison, who seemed to be assigned to him.

The barn was neat and clean. The stalls appeared to have good biting room. They were yet to find out just how much he liked to grab clothing. He had become famous in his previous locations for shooting his head out and turning it flat so he could get a better grip on mid-sections and other vital parts.

After one day in his new home, hip 769, soon to be named Clay County, was given an orange highway cone to warn off passersby. He took it as a badge of honor, and vowed to earn it.

I once read that no horse is so bad that it can't carry a dream. Our dream began anew each time we added a new horse to our stable.